The Hermit, by Charlotte Rodgers

The Heretic's Journey: Spiritual Freethinking for Difficult Times

by Steve Dee

The Universe Machine

The Heretic's Journey ©2018 Steve Dee

ISBN 978-0-9954904-7-5

All rights reserved. No part of this publication may be reproduced or transmitted in any form or by any means, electronic or mechanical, including photocopying, recording or by any information retrieval system without the prior written permission of the copyright owner, except for brief quotations in a review.

Original artwork: ©the artists

Editing, typesetting, and design: Nikki Wyrd

First published in July, 2018 by The Universe Machine, Norwich.

We are unraveling our navels so that we may ingest the sun.

We are not afraid of the darkness.

We trust that the moon shall guide us.

We are determining the future at this very moment.

We know that the heart is the philosopher's stone.

Our music is our alchemy.

    — Saul Williams, Coded Language, 2001

Contents

Foreword 1

Acknowledgements 5

Introduction 7

Shy Stories of Freedom 11

Queer Stories of Heresy 15

Heretic Heroes and Queer Lenses 21

    Beguines and Beghards 22

    Queer Readings 25

Cathars, Witches and Rebel Voices 29

    Exercise 1: Sculpting the Heretic's Altar 33

Growing-up Gnostic 37

The Agnostic Gnostic 41

    The Gnosis of Not Knowing 41

    Gnosis: So What? 44

Witchcraft as a Liberation Theology 49

    Cognitive Liberty 50

    The Dreaming of the Witch 52

Surreal Christology (Part 1): The Haunting 55

Surreal Christology (Part 2): The Mirror 59

Surreal Christology (Part 3): The Trickster 63

Surreal Christology (Part 4): The Androgyne 67

Collage, Magic and the Unconscious 73

    Exercise 2: The Witch's Collage 75

Playing with Queer Cut-ups 79

    Exercise 3: Cut-ups 83

Great Questions, Great Answers 85

Further Adventures in Ma'at Magick 91

Working with Recent Ancestors 95

Ma'at, Typhonic Strands and AMOOKOS 101

An Audience with Charlotte Rodgers 113

Wisdom in the Aeon of Maat 125

Thoughts on the Queerness of Gnosis 131

Androgynes: Then, Now and Not Yet 137

    Introduction 137

    Androgyny as Spiritual Ideal 142

    Exercise: Ardhanarishvara brain rewiring rite 147

Monstrous Alchemy 151

Surreal Witchcraft 155

A Puja for Heretical Heroes 161

Words Made Flesh 165

Bibliography 171

Foreword

This volume is, in many ways, a continuation from Steve's first solo book *A Gnostic's Progress*. As with his previous work, some of the writing here was brewed up in the cauldron of theblogofbaphomet.com, to which Steve is a prolific and celebrated contributor. In common with his first work, *The Heretic's Journey* is a heady mix of esoteric approaches resonating with the many influences that weave together to make Steve Dee the awesome magician that he is. Steve's appreciation and celebration of the work of others is vital to his creative cosmology, and is exemplified in this volume by the inclusion of an interview with artist and magical practitioner Charlotte Rogers.

Art is a major theme in this work, particularly surrealist art (the work of Leonora Carrington is discussed extensively). But it would be wrong to think that *The Heretic's Journey* is purely a theoretical text. True to his identity as a chaos magician, when we talk about art, then that's something to engage with and practise, as much as admire! Steve describes the process of making magical collages and presents the reader with plenty of other hands-on esoteric techniques. My personal favorite in this volume is the Ardhanarishvara Brain Rewiring Rite.

You'll find witches dancing in this text, alongside androgynous future spirits, early Christian Gnostics (folks like the Beguines and Cathars), Kabbalists, alchemists, Zen mediators and more! *The*

Heretic's Journey celebrates the chimeric deities that Steve loves (such as Baphomet and Abraxas) with writing that explores the clash, the confluence and the curious blending of what, at first, may seem wildly different varieties of occulture. What harmoniously unites these diverse esoteric flavours is our author's gentle, inclusive and curious attitude. In his professional life, Steve works at the pointy end of social services; holding space in family therapy and other settings, supporting those who are in crisis. He is a healer whose skillful approach helps people transform the tough times they find themselves in. In a similar manner, our author's compassionate and playful orientation takes us on a journey through a multiplicity of powerful characters, histories, methods and meditations.

The Heretic's Journey includes a history of the Ophidian gnosis; the interpenetrating occult currents of the Arcane and Magickal Order Of the Knights Of Shambhala (AMOOKOS), the futuristic Ma'atian magick of Soror Nema, and the Typhonian Ordo Templi Orientis. Steve describes how these magical currents have informed each other, presenting original research from the perspective of a practitioner.

What's so heretical in this journey? Steve Dee certainly values that form of Gnosticism identified by the early Christians as a desire for direct, personal experience of the divine. In this, our author and the gnostic Christians have common cause. Yet for Steve, spiritual exploration often comes through the body (via dance or martial arts). Those fleshy bodies, in which some

Gnostics would claim the spark of God is trapped, becomes instead our means of liberation.

Other heresies include the exploration of Queer identities; from the homoerotic reading of Christian iconography to the kinky polymorphous forms of the Trickster spirit. Then there are Steve's heretical ideas about aeonics; with Well-balanced Ma'at living in perfect harmony with Vengeful Horus.

In embracing the idea of heresy Steve pushes beyond the monolithic forms of Christianity, to find a place where the insights of that religion can be integrated as part of the broader spiritual process. In this respect it may be helpful to remember that in the ancient Pagan world there was no concept of 'heresy'. Rather the Greek word *hairesis*, from which 'heresy' is derived—the original meaning of which was 'selection'—meant simply a school of thought and not an erroneous and deleterious doctrine. A heretic, then, could be thought of as one who selects a way of thinking.

Given the centrality of the body to Steve's gnostic magic, *The Heretic's Journey* could be said to be a 'tantric' or 'left-hand path' text, one that calls to mind the principle of Tantric yoga: "That by which we fall is that by which we rise". This same principle appears in alchemy (another area that this book engages with), where base lead has the capacity to elevate itself into the gold of illumination. The amazing alchemy of this book is that it not only includes spiritual gold but a veritable Electrum Magicum (the fabled magical alloy made of all seven traditional planetary metals).

Steve's experimental and diverse approach doesn't offer easy, neat answers. He, and you dear Reader, are far too savvy for that. For while *The Heretic's Journey* may be a blending of magical paths it's also a questioning, open-ended voyage of discovery. Deeply metamodern, closer to the classic of 14th century Christian mysticism *The Cloud of Unknowing* than some prescriptive download of divine revelation. But that's okay; magic is a mystery, a weird world of delicious uncertainty as much as it is a process of revelation and empowerment. By acknowledging this Mystery, and critically turning our aspiration for illumination into real-life embodied praxis, we too can make the heretic's journey.

May the road rise to meet you!

> Julian Vayne
> Devon, June 2018

Acknowledgements

Many thanks to Julian, Nikki and Lyn for friendship and ongoing magical work.

To Mogg, Andrew, Mishlen and Lee for their constructive feedback and encouragement.

To Lloyd and Charlotte for their fabulous artwork.

To Mike Magee; many thanks for the historical perspective and continuing wild inspiration.

To Nema for manifesting the Aeon of Maat.

To all those Queer heretics past, present and future—keep it weird!

Introduction

Magicians are generally those people who are willing to get their hands dirty in their attempts to explore Mystery. Rather than trying to find easy answers that seek to reduce complexity, we seek transformation through actively working with the tensions and dualities that we experience in the universe and ourselves. It's probably fair to say that this work is demanding and perilous, but those of us marked to walk this path, the pursuit of some safer, more sedate means is no longer possible. We have heard the call of the Wyrd!

The complexity of life and our struggle to find meaning can take us to some weird places. When the answers handed to us by our forebears cease to ring true or fail to help us in answering destiny's call, then it is often our suffering that compels us to seek different answers.

To seek the dark, the mysterious and strange is to test the limits of what we know. We become cosmonauts who push themselves from the capsule's safety in order to experience a freedom from the gravitational pull of the ordinary and the normal. Such a journey asks us to confront the very real and existential dimensions that we experience in the face of the vast and the unknown. Rather than trying to minimize the sense of terror that we might encounter, the project of initiation encourages us to actively explore our sense of awe in the face of darkness and the uncertainty.

The rewards of such work can be deep and rich. Whether our awe is generated through viewing the terrible beauty of Nature or via exploration of the weird realm of the unconscious, as we step over the threshold of what we thought we knew, so new dimensions become accessible. Ours is a process of unlearning, where received truths are questioned so that new stories might be written.

Whether the Space we seek to explore is external or internal it asks bravery of us. In order to pursue the work of personal alchemy and spiritual transformation we must be willing to remain open and curious in the face of our own fear and reluctance to sacrifice. So often this work requires that we cultivate our ability to sit with paradox and that we relinquish certainties that no longer hold true.

The call to heroic deeds can feel like an insurmountable peak that we squint at and then despair at the cost it might demand. In this book I hope to provide you with a reflection on my own pursuit of bravery and the tools I have valued and evolved in reaching the goal of greater authenticity.

This is a book that seeks to provoke you to heresy! The territory I invite you to explore is that of the spiritual free thinker who is no longer satisfied with the easy answer. The literal definition of Heretic is "to choose"; to make a conscious and active choice rather than merely accepting an opinion due to it being espoused by the mainstream or by those in authority. To walk such a path is far from risk-free, but in my view the rewards of such self-sovereignty are powerful and profound. It is my hope that this work with act as a catalyst for your own exploration of your heretic self, and in that exploration you will experience the unfolding of who you truly are.

Such an unfolding can take time. The magical axiom "To Dare, To Know, To Will and To Keep Silent" for me points to a circular process of refinement where the daring Mage receives new insight, which when proven through practice is internalized (kept silent) so that this incubation gives birth to further development/ mutation.

This internal alchemy can birth things within us that at first seem monstrous. As our freethinking allows us to conceptualize and articulate ideas beyond the realms of orthodoxy, so we will be viewed as Monsters. Witches, Werewolves, Vampires and an assortment of other freak-labels were applied to those who questioned the limits of what we thought we knew.

While the mundane world may conspire to keep us small and within a form that makes its control of us more possible, as explorers of awakening we have a more formidable task ahead of us. Our initial response may be to flinch when we see the possibility of who our deepest self might become; these glimpses at the edges of sight may demand too much of us; too much sacrifice, too great a transformation. Dear traveller, be of stout heart! The inner genius of your daemon doesn't require that we reach the goal before the journey has begun; rather it asks of us the bravery to stop and consider who we might be.

My hope is that this book will provide you with some inspiration for your journey. That it will fire your resources, and awaken your bravery and a longing for something deeper.

Shy Stories of Freedom

Stories have power. We tell ourselves stories all day long. Stories about the past and what it meant, as well as stories of how we want the future to be.

Other people tell us stories as well. Media bombardment about what and how we should think: slow-bleed toxicity leaking into our systems as we seek some space to think our own thoughts and to live our own lives. Their desperate hands claw at us as we try to break the surface to gulp in the fresh air of our own freedom.

Michel Foucault knew about the power of the stories we tell. The big stories or meta-narratives that we get told, and tell ourselves, profoundly shape our beliefs about who we are and what we are worth. In fear of nuance and complexity, we create stories to help manage our fears, and pushing the source of our confusion outside of ourselves and as far away as possible! It's hard not to do this, but as we wake up to it, we can begin to explore the possibility of writing something new.

In his ground-breaking work with David Epston, the family therapist Michael White recognized that his clients were frequently bringing a particular set of stories into the therapy room. Because of the nature of his work, these stories tended to be "problem saturated narratives", ones that focused almost exclusively on the problems being experienced, and often bowing under the weight of medicalized diagnosis. In their evolution of Narrative Therapy, White and Epston sought to help people recover the lost, "shy" stories of function that were hidden. In helping people uncover these stories they helped them tap into forgotten veins of resilience.

The stories that constrain us are like the Gnostic Archons of old. They are spirits invested in inducing an amnesia that causes us to forget our true potential. They are the dusty layers that accrue on our Buddha Minds, impairing our ability to see and be seen for who we really are. These archonic tales make sense—of course they do! Otherwise we wouldn't pay them heed. Sadly they often play to our fears about the other, the different, and the new. They deal in certainties that downplay the detail and rely on the grouping together of humans and ideas, so that tidy labels can be applied.

Perhaps the first stage in recovering these shy stories is learning how to listen. Rather than anxiously projecting into the future or getting lost in the labyrinths of past "what ifs", what happens if we try to take in our current situation with a bit of Zen beginner's mind? Contemplative practices are good for this, allowing silence and space to turn down the volume on our endless narrative that we keep telling ourselves. This is not an easy place to start as the uncertainty and apparent emptiness can feel bewildering as we sit with things, rather than endlessly updating our internal status. If nothing else this is a good chance to do less and cultivate some curiosity: "What the hell is actually going on here?!"

Part of the power that big stories (meta-narratives as dominant discourses) hold over us is the sense of inevitability that they engender. These stories often like to fix identities and to locate qualities within groups or individuals rather than trying to understand the more complex interaction that occurs between ourselves, others and the social context we sit within. Yes, patterns can be reinforcing—e.g. you might bomb the shit out of people and they may get angry with you—but it doesn't follow that all those people are angry at all times and in all situations. Thankfully Systemic thinking and Narrative approaches (with all their postmodern subtlety) have some interesting ways of interacting with, and disrupting, such vicious circles.

In contrast with more Freudian approaches, rather than locating qualities within a given individual, Systemic and Narrative approaches are more interested in the dynamics between people, and the scripts and stories that are constructed as we interact within a variety of socio-political settings. Rather than being overly preoccupied with prying secret meaning from the depths of the unconscious, it seeks to explore new or lost meanings by being curious and Columbo-like about the way we communicate.

One technique that can open up such curiosity is that of externalization. If we tend to locate current challenges internally: "I am a failure" or "I am depressed", externalization invites us to decentralize the issue and enter into a dialogue with it. E.g. "How long has depression been affecting aspects of your life as a whole?" In working with this approach we might write letters to the given issue-

"Dear Book Buying habit...."

In writing we are not seeking a quick fix, rather we are seeking to explore both the negative and positive aspects of a given issue in our lives. Book buying might be connected to an academic pressure to know more than others, or it might represent more helpful urges towards self-development. By decentralizing issues that feel problematic, good Narrative practice then seeks to explore the space created. Are there other stories of function? Can we tune into shy skills and talents that have become buried by problem saturation?

To disrupt, decentre and externalize are processes innate to much of magical practice. Our engagement with spirits is a way of understanding and negotiating with differing aspects of ourselves. Things that we may want to exorcise and/or build pacts with. This is not to reduce them to mere psychological parlour tricks; rather it helps us understand the deeper motives for the alliances we seek. Those interested in this approach should check out the awesome work of Philip Farber, and Ramsey Dukes' *Little Book of Demons*.

To be a magician is to awaken to the narrative being told, both by ourselves and the cultures that shape us. We can't really turn the story off, but we can choose to slow the story down, listen more clearly and become more active in creating narrative rather than simply consuming those that others give to us. Don't let the Archons grind you down!

Queer Stories of Heresy

All of our stories are inevitably shaped by own contexts, genetic inheritance and the decisions that we feel we have had varying degrees of control over. Being the parent of two teenage humans has hugely affected my engagement with the world and they regularly ask questions that reflect the new eyes with which they view the world around them. Certainly in the realm of what it means to seek spiritual meaning, they have often proven to be quite thought provoking in asking me to articulate what I actually "believe" in terms of my own metaphysics. My eldest child helpfully summarized his take on my spiritual path as being "some sort of weird druid, meditation thing". I remember laughing at his response and while part of me would have wanted it to sound more impressive, I thought "Credit where credit is due, that's probably not far off!"

While I have had some past attempts at spiritual brand loyalty, they have habitually ended in consumer dissatisfaction. My path has always been a blurry one, a fuzzy inexact ramble along a path that is much more about exploration and the privilege of travelling with some rather excellent companions.

I can understand why others like certainty, and given the current scary state of Global politics, I can appreciate why such apparently vague, postmodern and Queer perspectives may not appear to be muscular enough to confront our current difficulties. While some may be frustrated by the complexity and multiplicity that that such perspectives bring to our construction of story, it seems to be part of my vocation as a magical practitioner to embody and verbalize such an approach.

To engage with Magic is to engage with the whole of life. It is art and it is science, it is acceptance and change. It is many things, but I'm pretty sure that it demands a heroic pursuit of curiosity and a willingness to question almost everything we thought was true of our lives and selves, as I have said elsewhere:

> *"Whatever else Magic may or may not accomplish it aims to transform our own awareness so that we become more effective. By self-willed mimetic infection, the change that we seek becomes more likely as we sensitize our perception to themes and opportunities."*

'Deep Chaos part deux' at
https://theblogofbaphomet.com

To enter the circle or to cast a spell means to lift anchor on what we thought we knew about ourselves. Whatever scripts and stories that we may have inherited about what our lives should look like, are called into question as we sail more uncertain seas. We are entering Queer territory!

Part of why I view my own magic as Queer (as well as it being poured through the life of a Kinky, Bisexual and gender fluid person), is the way in which I consider that Queerness embodies the role that we as magicians have as edge-dwellers who question oppressive categorization and help pull our cultures forward.

Queer Stories of Heresy

Queer is by definition whatever is at odds with the normal, the legitimate, the dominant. There is nothing in particular to which it necessarily refers. It is an identity without an essence. 'Queer' then, demarcates not a positivity but a positionality vis-à-vis the normative.

David Halperin, *Saint Foucault: Towards a Gay Hagiography*

Queer discourse

Some may find the descriptor "Queer" problematic because of its historic associations as a homophobic slur or because it is viewed as attempting to summarize the complex terrain of "non-straight" identity (LGBT+) with a single (albeit complex) word. I certainly don't wish to imply any form of flatland homogenization of people's lives and politics. Language and self-identification are important markers and means for both self-understanding, and collective response.

17

While some view the conscious deconstruction of category as being overly hip or laboured, for those of us who find liberty within Queer's punk rock attitude, Queerness challenges us to experience relationship and uncertainty in new ways. Rule books that rely on clear categorization and the safe assertion that problems are located in "the other" can no longer be as true. While the urge for individual emancipation and freedom seem innate to the human project, a Queer awakening might also attend to the complex tendrils of connectivity between self and other. Indeed our liberty may ultimately be within context as much as it is about liberation away from it.

Whichever framework one employs in trying to understand how Magic works, most magicians seem to rely on concepts of connection, alliance and symbiosis. Over 20 years of frontline social work may have well and truly kicked most naïvety out of my system, but I still know that my own Magic seems to be maximized when I have the possibility of exploring creativity from a position of flexibility and relative fearlessness. It's hard for me to reconcile such freedom and connection with a siege mentality that imagines safety behind a balsa-wood drawbridge. However much we may need to create a temporary autonomous zone in which we can rediscover our own story and voice, in my view we must also risk connection so that our spirituality can be proven and move beyond solipsism.

As a self-defining Witch and magical practitioner, these themes seek an outworking within a ritual space. In recent times I have been working with the Goddess Sophia and the way she is made manifest in Gaia. In offering devotional practice to Gaia-Sophia, my coven-mates and I have been seeking to explore means of experiencing greater connectivity and Wisdom. This prayer from our work together remains on my lips and at the forefront of my mind:

> Praise to the Wise one,
> The Connected One,
> The Whole one,
> The Holy One!
> Gaia-Sophia!
> Sublime Strange Attractor-
> Illuminate our intuition and give us neither-neither genius!
> Help us to spin our webs of connection with silver and gold
> Help us to seek Wisdom and apply its insights with kindness.
> We give thanks to you and to each other
> For this time of nurture and deep listening!

Heretic Heroes and Queer Lenses

Queer theory can not only shape aspects of our magical practice, it can provide us with a lens that can profoundly impact on the way we may choose to read and use history in finding inspiration for our spiritual journeys. I have always been a bit of a history geek and was in a definite minority as a theology undergraduate in wanting to dig into the way in which personality and politics intersected in the human attempt to find religious meaning. While others may have viewed the early Gnostics or the pre-Whitby Celtic Church as dull, I dug deep into these ecclesiastical detective stories as they provided such a rich resource for understanding the questions that I was personally engaged with.

The reading of any text is a complex process in which the information provided is inevitably shaped by the worldview of the reader. This awareness of how our own perspectives or "presupposition pool" influences our interpretation is central to the field of hermeneutics. While hermeneutics originally developed in relation to the understanding of biblical and other sacred texts, its insights were eventually adopted in a broad range of human sciences, and its philosophical implications were explored by philosophical figures as august as Heidegger and Hans-Georg Gadamer.

We are all engaged in hermeneutics, and our own biases and contexts inevitably shape the 'lens' through which we seek to make sense of something. What hermeneutics has been hugely helpful in making historians more aware of, are the dangers that our readings might face if we are less conscious of how our own biases and contexts impact on our explorations.

In my recent explorations of Gnosticism, and religious freethinking more generally, I have been increasingly aware of my own lens as a person who identifies with many aspects of Queer identity. When one is trying to comprehend how a person's Queerness might shape their process of interpretation we have to acknowledge that we are already contending with a highly fluid concept that defines itself by its ability to defy easy categorization. That being said, the experience that I have as a reader of religious history is one in which my own experience as a sexual and gender outsider sensitizes me to similar themes that I empathically sense within the narratives with which I am engaging.

Now this all sounds very heady, so it might be helpful to provide an example of how something has recently inspired me and how my context has shaped the themes that have emerged.

Beguines and Beghards

I'll start by stating that the spiritual movement of the Beguines—and their male counterparts the Beghards—is impossible to summarize succinctly, given the diversity of their geographical contexts and the historical time span during which their movement was most vibrant. For more information I would recommend books such as *Beguine Spirituality* by Fiona Bowie, and the more recent *The Wisdom of the Beguines* by Laura Swan.

Heretic Heroes and Queer Lenses

Not nuns

In summary, the Beguines were a network of predominantly female lay communities that sought to pursue their own sense of vocation outside of formal monastic rules and orders. The golden age of the Beguines was between the 12th and 16th centuries, and their communal houses (Beguinages) thrived most readily in the Low Countries of Europe, the area including Belgium, the Netherlands, and bordering on France and Germany.

While the Beguines were devoted to the monastic ideals of celibacy and simple living, each house was free to evolve its own rule, and these communities were noted for their continued involvement in commerce (especially the textile trade) as a means of supporting themselves. They were noted mystics who placed a high value on visionary experience, and some scholars have noted the influence of the troubadour and courtly love traditions in relation to their passionate longing for union with the beloved.

As with so many radical and visionary groups in the medieval period, the Beguines aroused a decidedly mixed response from those in authority. While they were initially seen as embodying a high level of piety, the rate at which women joined the communities was seen as a threat to male power and control.

The Beguines had not submitted a common rule for Papal approval, and their emphasis on mystical experience almost inevitably drew accusations of heresy. They received Papal condemnation in 1311 and in the previous year, one of their most outspoken leaders Marguerite Porete was burnt at the stake for failing to renounce her visionary work *The Mirror of Simple Souls*. Despite their devout lives, church authorities saw connections between the Beguines and more overtly antinomian groups, such as the Brethren of the Free Spirit.

In subsequent centuries the Beguines underwent several waves of renewal and rehabilitation, but the Reformation, and the decline of the textile trade (their main source of income), eventually contributed to their numbers diminishing. While the anti-monastic agenda of the Reformation inevitably impacted on the Beguines, their continued involvement in health care and education provided them with an important social function; Beguine communities continued in Belgium until the early part of the 20th century.

Queer Readings

My Queer reading of this history occurs at a number of levels and undoubtedly has considerable intersects with both Feminist and Anarchist readings of Beguine history. While my own lack of Christian faith may inevitably create some metaphysical distance between my and their spiritual experience, there is still much that I connect with. Here are some of the primary themes that emerged in my engagement with them:

- Organizational liberty. The Beguines inspire me in their determined rejection of centralized authority. While they situate themselves firmly within the pre-Reformation Catholic faith, their desire to shape their own paths at a local and communal level has many connections to the way Queer activism challenges us to pursue social change.
- Personal gnosis. While the religious language of their society was still core to Beguine experience, in the face of male dominance in the Priesthood and other Ecclesiastical domains they found power and self-definition through visionary experience. Similarly, Queer identity—while using the language of culture regarding orientation and gender—retains the right of the individual to blur and play with these concepts in order to locate a 'best-fit' version of self.
- Rejection of heteronormativity and an increase in Female Power. The Beguines freaked the church out! These women found a collective means for self-definition and a rejection of potentially endless, life-threatening reproduction. Themes

around an increase of female power were also vital to Gnostic groups such as the Cathars during the same period, and the threat that these groups posed to male dominance was a likely catalyst to the later witch trials of the Early Modern period.

Beginning to do it for themselves

Such reflections are far from definitive, and are presented as serving suggestions as to how Queer (or other) lenses might be employed. The conscious use of such approaches can be hugely inspiring, and my own engagement with groups such as the Beguines are part of my own personal explorations of themes as diverse as New Monasticism and the impact of Christian heresy on Witchcraft traditions. The viewing of old history with a fresh set of eyes can provide us with rich veins of new material.

Cathars, Witches and Rebel Voices

In seeking to view historic sources of inspiration with new eyes, the Cathars have always proved to be something of an enigma. While on one level they provide a vivid example of how Gnostic religion survived into the medieval period, it can still be problematic trying to discern what they did and did not believe. This is partly due to history often belonging to the most powerful, i.e. the Church and the Inquisition, but it may also reflect a religious tradition more focused on a living encounter with mystery, rather than codifying a systematic theology.

Cathar cross

What does seem clear about them, is that they were incredibly courageous in being willing to question the orthodoxies that the Church and State were hugely invested in maintaining. As with the Gnostics of antiquity, Cathar theology seems to have been derived from an encounter with a God who seemed irreconcilable

29

with the material realm. The stark realities of human pain and impermanence led to them adopting a worldview that was a radical inversion of Church teaching.

The Cathars' dualism meant a rejection of the creator God. By extension they rejected the Church teaching that the project of marriage and reproduction was actually a good idea. If your view is that the material realm needs to be escaped from, then the entrapment of even more spiritual beings tends to not be viewed positively. Not only were the Cathar Perfecti clear in their rejection of sexual activity that could lead to childbirth, they viewed marriage itself as negative and were accused by the church as advocating abortion.

The historic connection between the Cathars and the Bulgarian Bogomils is fairly well attested, and the accusation of the latter group engaging in "buggery" and other forms of non-reproductive sexual activity may have some credence beyond mere slander. The terms Bogomil originally meant "Friend of God", but those threatened by their Gnostic teachings were so persistent in their accusations of sodomy, that the group became synonymous with anal activity. It may well be difficult to ascertain whether the Perfecti themselves were absolute celibates, but it seems probable that an engagement in non-penis in vagina sex in the wider Cathar church was consistent with their desire to avoid pregnancy.

Whatever one makes of their dualism, it's fascinating to consider how these themes of inversion and the unnatural became central to not only the persecution of heretical groups such as the Beguines, Cathars and the Brethren of the Free Spirit, but also how such concepts contributed to the perception of Medieval Witchcraft. As Norman Cohn has rightly highlighted, the accusations brought against the alleged practitioners of Witchcraft are as old as time its self. Accusations of sexual depravity, cannibalism and abortion are the stock-in-trade for those in power wanting to depict a religious minority as being the hidden cause of societal unrest. Jews, Christians, Gnostics and practitioners of Magic have all been persecuted on the basis that they engaged in such activities and that their practice of such unnatural inversions is a direct threat to the well-being of the masses. Such acts of depravity either promoted the presence of disorder and disease e.g. the Black Death, or they invited divine retribution due to the failure to eradicate such miscreants.

What seems fairly clear is the manner in which minority groups such the Cathars and those accused of Witchcraft became a location onto which the fantasies and fears of those in power could be projected. Whether it was the imagined orgies of Witches at the Sabbat, or Cathars having lots of Queer sex, their status as outsiders, without real power and recourse to stable judicial process, made them highly vulnerable to persecution. Sadly, history confirms that such strategies of distancing and demonizing make it easier for the powerful to view such minority communities as dangerous, threatening and therefore disposable and warranting of savagery.

The threat that we as spiritual freethinkers represent is a pushing at the boundaries of what is currently deemed right and at times lawful by those who hold power. Such authority is usually based on the fiction that ethics and values are fixed rather than evolving, and that if we question the norm, then our motivation must be to cause harm.

The Witch and Heretic will inevitably be those figures viewed as anarchic and antinomian and while those who embrace those descriptors know that's only part of the story, we may consciously revel in the disruption they provoke. As outsiders we are sensitized to power, both its use and misuse.

For most of us, the pursuit of spiritual paths that involve magic and gnosis entails a direct challenge to the forms of reality that the mainstream wants us to accept. We are the inverts, the Queer and the outsiders seeking to push forward the liminal edge of our cultures, so that they may evolve and that we may have space to thrive. I do not reject nature and the wild beauty of our world, but I continue to question concepts of what it means to be "natural" within it. Concepts of fixity and desires for a romantic stone age should be open to questioning and as a heretical freethinker I will continue to do so.

While some occultists may sneer at the way that the Witch as truth-teller has been co-opted by the so-called "liberal agenda" (like that's such a bad thing?) events in Poland in 2016 provided us with a powerful example of how these archetypes could act as triggers for liberation. In being faced with a parliament hell-bent on implementing draconian laws aimed at further restricting Women's access to safe and legal abortions, the Witches took to the streets. Thousands of black-clad (predominantly women) activists downed tools and protested as a potent and defiant "fuck

Cathars, Witches and Rebel Voices

you" to those who sought to further their control. While the battle for religious and reproductive liberty is ongoing, I couldn't help but smile and be inspired at a social media post by a Polish friend of mine who had taken part:

"We are the granddaughters of all the Witches you were never able to burn."

Never again the burning times

Exercise 1: Sculpting the Heretic's Altar

One of the techniques that I employ during my day-job as a Systemic or Family Psychotherapist is that of the sculpt. Sculpting is a tool for making an external picture, or 'sculpt', of an internal process such as feelings, experiences, or perceptions. It can use objects and bodily postures as way of experimenting with the relationship between things and how their proximity or distance might express the dynamics of communication and power.

In this activity I am proposing that we create an altar as a means for exploring the interplay between different aspects of our heretical selves. Religious or spiritual altars often express something of our aspirations and longings, and it is interesting to note the changes we make to them (or the time we spend in front of them) depending on which guiding principles or realities we wish to experience more of.

The first part of our tasks is to collect a series of objects, pictures and texts that embody those heretical, rebellious and inspirational figures and ideas that mark us as outsiders and inspire our processes of free thought. At this point it is important that we don't overthink this process. We won't be looking at our neighbour's altar to see who has assembled the hippest pantheon!

We may draw our inspiration from a broad spectrum or it may reflect the narrowness of our current obsessions. In my case I had everything from an icon of St Francis, a Gurdjieff book, a leather-clad Cat woman figurine and a Henry Rollins CD. I made little attempt to rationalize why I needed this collection of heretic heroes together, I was simply aware that they embodied important markers in my own journey of personal liberation.

As a person with strong devotional tendencies, I then spent some time offering incense to the assembled representation of free-thinking, before undertaking my normal meditative practice. This felt less an act of worship and more a process of acknowledging and aligning myself with those embodiments of freedom.

If you choose to undertake this task, I would recommend an initial period of simply "sitting with" the choices that you have made. Maybe note their presence and position within a journal or magical diary so that any future changes can be noticed.

Working with sculpts can be accomplished in many ways, and it may be interesting to note how this altar-sculpt evolves over time. You may want to shift the objects to change their proximity to each other (interestingly Cat Woman now seems to be whipping St. Francis; but it looks consensual!) or we may want to introduce new elements to either maximize a component or to provide a sensed need for counterbalance (in my case a black feather representing Ma'at).

However you chose to work with this exercise, as with most sculpts, the aim is to externalize those key aspects of who we are so that in seeing them "out there", we can gain a greater sense of clarity having brought them more fully into the more conscious parts of self. The purpose of beginning such work is usually far more beneficial if we view it as an unfolding process of questioning and exploration for ourselves rather than attempting to rush towards answers prematurely.

Growing-up Gnostic

Most spiritual paths seem to have as part of their focus a desire to help us create a sense of certainty and security as we try to engage with the challenging messiness of human experience. Whether via the provision of a coherent world view or at least a set of practices that help provide meaning and alleviate boredom, religions of various stripes work hard at trying to create a buffer between ourselves and the existential anxiety that appears to be innate to our shared humanity.

One of the core questions that Gnosticism seeks to grapple with is whether the religious answers that we seek are real solutions, or whether they are more likely to perpetuate a sleepy engagement with a world that actually needs answers with a sharper edge. Do our attempts at meaning help us grow to our full potential as human beings; or do they sustain a child-like dependence and immaturity?

Scott Peck in *A Different Drum* sought to identify the various developmental stages that a person might go through as they try to grow within their chosen world view. Peck saw an adherence to formal/institutional forms of faith as being quite childlike in its desire for certainty. To remain in this state requires a degree of blinkeredness in shutting off new information that might be viewed as introducing unnecessary confusion. These believers may well deal with high levels of stress and complexity in other areas of their lives, but in the realm of metaphysics and faith, dependence and clarity are vital.

In contrast with the position of the child, the rebellious adolescent is perpetually sceptical and questioning. This highly individualistic perspective, imbued with rebellion and punk rock energy, seeks to actively deconstruct those literal, less critical versions of belief that they formerly embraced. While this approach might be ideal for generating heresy and polemic, it may not be so great at sustaining an enterprise.

For Peck the more mature, integrated adult position is that of the Mystic who is able to approach the mythic richness of a given faith with a more nuanced and communal perspective. The questioning of the rebel is retained, but their sceptical energy is directed at trying to access a richer, more archetypal appreciation of stories that were once scorned. The exploration of spiritual meaning will (by necessity) have a more collaborative dimension, in which we allow our relationships to support us in tolerating uncertainty and allowing us to explore greater psychological openness.

The Gnostics were keen to push us toward this more adult position, challenging us to adopt radical reinterpretations of biblical myth triggered by a daring trust in personal religious insight (Gnosis). In their perception of humanity's core dilemma, the Gnostics also mapped out a three-fold schema of the differing responses that people gave. In contrast to the *hylic's* coarse materialism and the *psychic's* inability to rise above their immediate context, the *pneumatic* aims of the Gnostics asked them to seek a spiritual dimension (the divine spark) that transcended the sensory bombardment and impermanence of the material world.

While the Gnostics were frequently startling in the originality of their vision, it would seem fair to ask whether their approach was simply too stark and demanding a path to follow. If this is growing up, do I even want to?

To be fair to the Gnostics they never claimed that life was easy or that their path was universal. To reflect on impermanence and the path of liberation necessitates a greater awareness of the tricky nature of reality, and the lack of fulfilment that our current paths are providing. To seek Gnosis as a means of greater freedom will always involve risk and the possibility of rejection by those seeking more orthodox answers.

Recent commentators on the Gnostic revival (e.g. Stephan Hoeller and Hans Jonas) have been keen to point out the similarities between the aims of the Gnosticism and the philosophical pursuits of existentialism. In struggling to find coherent meaning in our experience of life, the existentialists often proposed a heroic engagement with uncertainty, and an exploration of how personal action into the world might affect it. Each of these paths seem to be pointing to a place where our struggle with meaning asks us to take responsibility for the path we take. As the existential psychologist Rollo May observed, "courage is not the absence of despair; it is, rather the capacity to move ahead in spite of despair". (*The Courage to Create*)

The call "to put away childish things" will have different implications for all of us. For me this call to adulthood is not one in which playfulness or simplicity are abandoned, rather it presents a challenge to stop expecting spoon-fed answers. Nor, to pay too much attention to my own inner-parent's demands that my current path is not quite good enough ("meditate more, acquire more information!").

Unlike the moody rebel this path is not one of arid isolation and false independence. As much as this path is uniquely my own, I gain much from the company and encouragement of others. The connections that I make and sustain are hopefully more shaped by shared adulthood and the desire to co-create; and while I continue to respect and seek counsel from those further along the path, I no longer expect them to have the answers that only my own internal alchemy can produce.

The Agnostic Gnostic

I count myself fortunate to have a small number of close friends who can ask me challenging questions in a respectful but fairly direct manner. One such friend having read my previous book *A Gnostic's Progress* had some pointy inquiries about how could we really know anything, and whether the pursuit of such occult know-how was ultimately a distraction from the real business of the here and now. He wondered whether, given the various twists and turns that my spiritual journey has taken, would I want an answer to my seemingly endless questioning? Would I even know what an answer looked like if I arrived at one?

These are great questions and while I may not have immediate or complete answers, I thought it would be of value to reflect on them. In seeking to engage them, rather than seeking to wrestle with them via direct confrontation, what I will attempt is more an Aikido like side-step slightly out of the way so as to move with the energy of the challenge they may represent.

The Gnosis of Not Knowing

"If you are a Gnostic, then shouldn't you know stuff?"

This is a good question and you might rightly wonder why anyone would pursue a gnostic path if they didn't end up knowing more. Paradoxically however, when I try to compare the nature of what I know now, compared to what I thought I knew when I was following a faith-based path, I am fairly sure that I am less certain about a whole range of things!

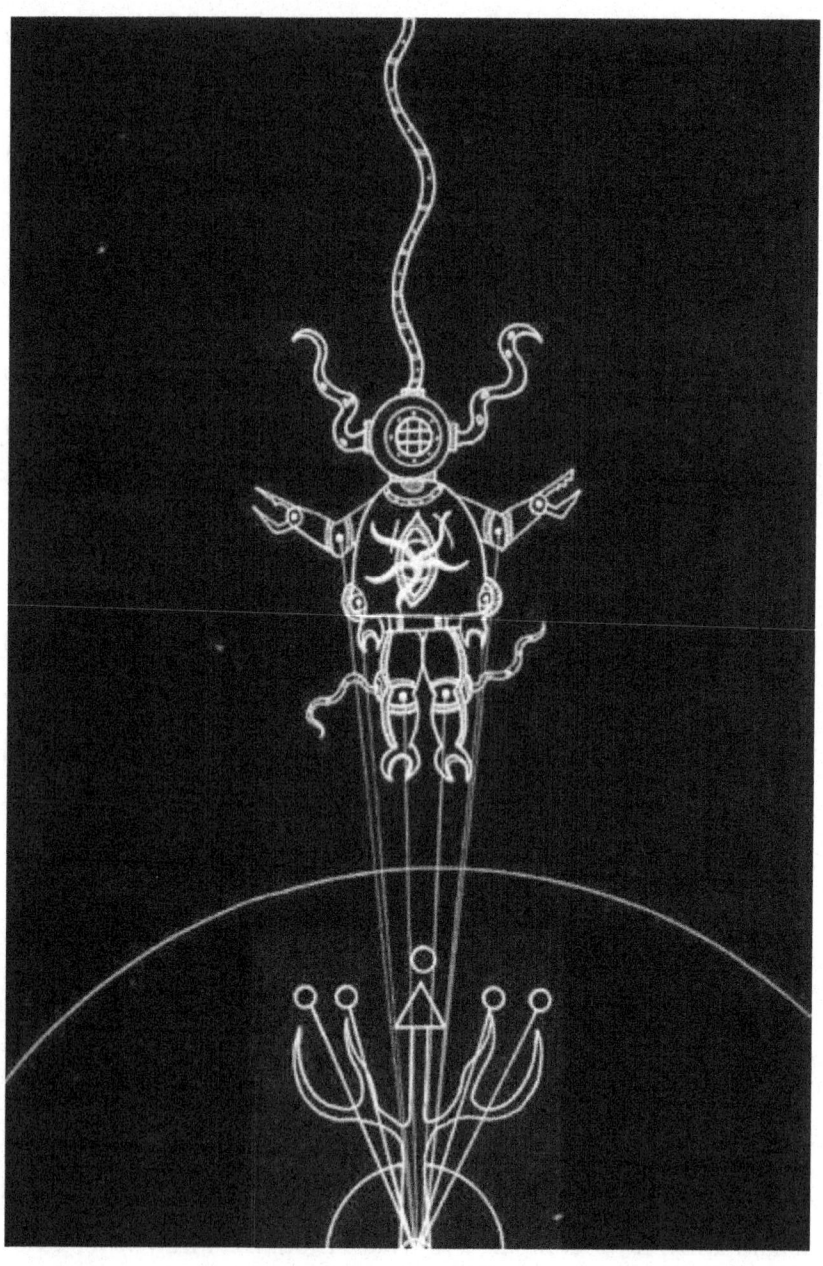

Watcher, Lloyd Keane

The Agnostic Gnostic

Part of my ongoing fascination with the Gnostic current is the way in which it seeks to grapple with the unknown. Its vivid myths are replete with alien gods and mysterious realms that defy description. As human beings look up at the night sky or plumb the depths of dark seas, we are confronted (and potentially terrified) by mystery. We can of course aspire, through our science and art, to gain greater understanding of the hidden dimensions of what's out there (or indeed in here), but this process of self-reflection and wondering is arguably an essential part of our experience of consciousness.

It seems important at this juncture to recognize the potential dangers of basing our perspectives on what the psychotherapist Barry Mason might call "unsafe certainty", a type of certainty based on absolutes that struggles with new information and insights. Often it feels that my great moments of Gnosis or Insight relate to the potential limits to what I can and can't know.

While the historic Gnostics were somewhat renowned for their complex cosmologies with multiple layers inhabited by a multitude of beings, for me the value of such perspectives is far less about adopting weirder world views, and far more about using them to help access a greater sense of cognitive liberty. My own experience of trying to work with the Gnostic myths has had some similarity to Zen koan study inasmuch as the difficulty in trying to comprehend these schemas intellectually, has driven me towards a sense of knowing that seems to occur at a deeper, more integrated level.

The gaining of such insight is rarely a straight line, once-for-always experience; rather it is a spiralling process where one has moments of internal spaciousness that come in and out of view as we live our lives. Famously, the Zen practitioner seeks to engage in their endeavours with "Great Faith, Great Doubt and Great Courage". Given that Zen Buddhist practice is generally less preoccupied with externalized metaphysical preoccupations, the emphasis on Great Faith is often seen as relating to faith or belief in the process of our own practice in relationship with both teacher and Sangha (community). My own journey into working with the Gnostic tradition has similarly been focused on strengthening or cultivating my ability to receive new information while simultaneously using doubt and questioning as tools to unburden myself from perspectives that are now outdated. This is also where Great Courage comes in! If we no longer believe in the certainties of a given orthodoxy and we seek to place greater value on the process of personal spiritual insight, then we are quite radically asking people to take far greater responsibility for themselves. Some people frankly can't handle this, especially if they experience their faith-based certainties as being an effective means of protection from life's messiness.

Gnosis: So What?

In thinking about the contemporary value of Gnosticism as a vital spiritual impulse, while the role of heretic may well be essential to catalyse our initial push into spiritual free-thinking, if we are to develop maturity it is also important to move beyond the role of being an endlessly ranting rebel. This may entail the relinquishing of outdated certainties and a move towards "safe uncertainty" that seems to necessitate a greater awareness, of what is arising in the moment, as well as our need for relationships that nurture. In short, if belief in dogma no longer provides any guarantee of insight, we may need to be more discerning/demanding of what behaviour you would hope to see (for yourself and others) if genuine gnostic revelation has occurred.

In reflecting on the current shape of those groups and organizations that are claiming connection to historic Gnosticism, it seems significant that many of these bodies have a greater emphasis on the use of either sacraments or collective ritual practice. In contrast to cultures shaped by a Protestant emphasis on intellectual ascent to the dogma of creedal statements and scriptural authorities, those groups have a greater emphasis on the lived practice of ritual activity to provide containment and guidance for their gnostic experience. For the flame of radical subjectivity to be nurtured and sustained, these shared rites arguably provide communal markers through which experiences can be triangulated and matured.

Explorer, Lloyd Keane

Perhaps this emphasis on practice and relationship gets closer to the heart of what it means to really know. Gnosis is just the beginning, a spark if you will that then needs to be tended. A good fire needs not only a source/spark, but also fuel and oxygen. For the Gnostic explorer to experience their insight as more sustaining, the spark of insight needs to be used and fed. This is a circular process in which we offer something to others and also acknowledge our need to receive. This reciprocal dynamic may entail the making of meals, the creation of Art, spending time listening, and so the list goes on. I can have endless amounts of weird shit going on in my head but unless I use it to do (whether for myself and others), then we would be right to question its ultimate value.

Witchcraft as a Liberation Theology

Most religious systems are ultimately designed as systems of liberation. They may differ in terms of what they think we are in need of liberation from (Sin, Desire, Ignorance, Maya etc.), but my own reading is that they are seeking to offer some sort of solution to our haunting sense of discomfort.

While such answers may begin with the insights of an enlightened individual, they rarely remain as such. Given time to evolve and gaze outwards, many religious traditions develop a Mahayanist/social dimension where the liberation of the individual demands a response to the "other"; other beings and the cosmos more generally. While developments such as Bodhisattva vows and states of kenosis (self-emptying) are no guarantee of socio-political engagement, if they can avoid the pit-fall of paternalism, they can often provide the basis for developing more empowered notions of interdependence and systemic awareness.

The 1950s and '60s witnessed an important movement within the Roman Catholic Church in South America, when people who were engaged with the coal face of day-to-day hardship, re-envisioned the gospel message in relation to political and economic oppression. The Liberation of the Israelites from Egypt and the Gospel message of Christ were viewed as narratives of freedom whereby "the downtrodden were lifted up" (Luke 1:52). With the birth of Liberation Theology in the works of Boff, Gutierrez et al, past dogmas were no longer sufficient, and the rigors of true discipleship were now to be measured in terms of deeds or praxis. As Desmond Tutu powerfully observed; "If you are neutral in situations of injustice, then you have chosen the side of the oppressor."

In seeking to reflect on the importance of my historical forbears as an aspiring heretic, I've been wondering again about the relationship between liberation and this thing we call 'Witchcraft'. What does Witchcraft claim to offer liberation from? And is it able to embrace or embody liberation at a collective level?

Much ink has been spilt in attempting to define what Witchcraft may or may not have been, and while we may have re-appropriated it from accusing lips, its evocative potency evades concrete categorization.

Cognitive Liberty

In his *Europe's Inner Demons*, Norman Cohn masterfully analyses the evidence with regard to the likelihood of the Witches' Sabbath having any basis in historic fact. Cohn concludes that it was highly unlikely that the fevered imaginings of persecuting clerics had any foundation in relation to some sort of denominational adherence to a set of pan-European 'night ecstasies'. What seems more evident is that their actions were overwhelmingly directed at other groups of people who still considered themselves Christians. While it is almost inevitable that some of these Christians practiced magic (and by doing so, demonstrated their humanity), the fear projected by these clerics was more often motivated by an ungodly desire to control.

The Church's ability to control would always be challenged by the heterodoxy of groups such as the Cathars, the Brethren of the Free Spirit and the Beguines, the power of their subjective gnostic experiences being valued above any external authority. Whatever the degree of adherence to such beliefs by the mainstream of society, the ideas that such outsider groups represented embodied a type of cognitive liberty that eroded the hold of any centralized hegemony.

While we may not buy into Michelet's idealization of the Witch as Satanic freedom fighter, there is something subversive contained within even the simplest act of folk magic. To express a sense of agency through a magical act that uses means outside or beyond the Church's recognized sacraments is to commit an act of heteropraxy and defiance.

Within the collective psyche of Europe, the Witch has often acted as an icon of disturbance and freedom. The projected fantasies of clerics and folkloric imaginings allude to something dark, disturbing and subversive. The Witch acts as an attractor for the shadow aspects of those cultures within which they are suspected of dwelling. They are the hags and the shape-shifters whose messy bodies simultaneously arouse and unsettle us. They seem to be scapegoats onto whose heads the repressed longings of society are spoken.

In bearing the weight of such dangerous passions they hold a position on the outer edge of social and ethical evolution. In seeking to own their own sense of spiritual and moral agency, it could be argued that magicians have played a catalysing role in pushing the boundaries of moral acceptability. When we consider a figure like Crowley and his impact on 20th century culture, while his personal chaos may still make him less than attractive as a role model, his bisexuality and entheogenic exploration that then caused such outrage are now arguably far less contentious due to his bravery in seeking to live a more authentic life.

The Dreaming of the Witch

While scholars and practitioners may continue to debate the degree to which the transcripts of the Witch trials can be viewed as axiomatic in relation to what Witches actually did, they do seem to highlight the centrality of dreaming to what Witches did.

To travel to the Sabbat was to enter the realm of dreams. We might to choose to frame this as a form of astral travel or a salve-induced hypnopompic experience, but it seems that to be a Witch meant that the night-time became a liminal zone in which the fuzzy edges of consciousness were utilized for the work of magic.

Dreams can be viewed as having a multitude of meanings, but in brief we might summarize these key dimensions that I suspect most reflective types would agree upon:

1. They allow expression of unconscious material: We are bombarded with so much information in our waking hours that it is inevitable we should prioritize those things that are most essential or most palatable. The things we discard or suppress are often thrown into the depths of the unconscious

dimensions of self. During the various cycles of sleep, the filters between the conscious and unconscious are more permeable and unconsidered material may make new demands for our attention via dreams.

2. They are weird: Given that the unconscious is more of a swirling vortex than a neat filing system, the stuff that bubbles to the surface in our dreams can be decidedly odd. Linear time and clear correspondence are abandoned and the raw material of our dreams can be entertaining, confusing or terrifying.

3. They are often aspirational: While their strangeness and apparent disorganization defies most attempts to use them as maps in the usual sense, they can provide us with glimpses of possibility. If we accept that we are in a process of seeking to find meaning and some form of integration, then dreams can provide a potent means of trying to establish communication with the unconscious. Their bizarreness and fluidity can provide us with inspiration and insight that reason alone might not allow.

The dreaming of the Witches can provide a powerful and potentially disturbing means for fuelling and directing the processes of change within the culture they enchant.

As we have seen in considering our historical heroes, to question orthodoxies and seek new means for personal exploration will inevitably threaten those for whom stability is paramount. Those who have consciously embraced identities such as 'Witch', 'Magician' or 'Gnostic' have regularly aided our cultures' development, by prodding them to embrace diversity, multiplicity and liberty. When we take on this mantle for ourselves, we must remain awake to the reality that we represent; the freedom that so many seek, and that we still risk being scapegoated by those who would seek to maintain control.

Surreal Christology (Part 1): The Haunting

Have you ever felt haunted? Haunted by an idea or a person who, despite all your best efforts, seems to be lurking at the edges of your vision and prodding your unconscious to give them a bit more space. These phantoms of our history often point towards past explorations and adventures that were left unresolved; untidy longings that may seem embarrassing when viewed from a more urbane present.

In all my recent writing about the Gnostics and other Christian heretics, the figure haunting me from the shadows is that old trickster Yeshua Ben Joseph (or Jesus, to his Greek speaking friends). It may well be a projection on my part, but in my mind Jesus and I are trying to negotiate a different kind of relationship. Those dusty half-truths from fan-boys of old simply don't fit any more. Rather than taking shape within a dogma that does violence to either kindness or thinking, I keep getting glimpses of this Jesus in the dreamtime and the strangest of places. This is a decidedly Surreal Christology.

It is hardly surprising that Surrealism's emphasis on the unconscious and the realm of dreams coincided historically with the birth of psychotherapy and fin de siècle occultism. The sense of mystery and strange juxtaposition that are synonymous with

Surrealism have helped me to explore aspects of my spiritual history that I had previously felt unable to reconcile.

In considering Crowley's definition of Magick as being "The Art and Science of causing change in accordance with Will", I will acknowledge my own personal bias towards the art end of this equation. Surrealism as an artistic movement manages to capture the creativity and willed engagement with the unconscious that was later embodied so potently in the work of occult artists as diverse as Austin Osman Spare and Thee Temple of Psychick Youth. Such art revels in the conscious distortion of the familiar as we push up against the fuzzy edges of the known and the knowable (think melting clocks and fish on bicycles). Such an approach is radically subjective and relational, but uses images in a way that connects to shared meaning so as to provoke new ways of perceiving and understanding:

> *Artist, you are a priest: Art is the great mystery and, when your effort leads to a masterpiece, a ray of the divine shines down as on an altar... Artist, you are a magus. Art is the great miracle and proves our own immortality.*
>
> – Joséphin Péladan

Surrealist artists such as the fabulous Leonora Carrington (1917–2011) took this emphasis on the magical and alchemical a step further than most of her male forebears, and her work remains a potent example of the surreal genius engaging with the spiritual realm.

Whichever occult tools we think we may have mastered as we enter the faery realm of sleep, we soon realize that we are riding on waves of unconscious that are ultimately beyond our control. The esoteric skills of automatic writing and dream interpretation (methods which the Surrealists employed) may be effective vehicles for entering these waters, but we must still realize the limited control that we finally have over what creatures emerge from its depths!

I would highly recommend the use of Surrealist art (especially Carrington's and Max Ernst's) as an aid to meditation and reflection. The Surreal landscapes encountered via dreams and our art can be challenging and uncomfortable, but their jarring and vivid images can trigger awakenings more potent than if we were relying on words or reason alone.

My own departure from Christianity came following a profound psychological crisis in which I was no longer able to tolerate the exclusivity of that religion's claims. My book *A Gnostic's Progress* looks at this experience in greater detail, but it would be fair to summarize the direction of this journey as being inwards in search of greater, more authentic depth; a move away from faith-based belief, and towards an acceptance of responsibility for insights gained.

This journey inwards was greatly aided by the works of Jung, and it was via his work that I encountered the richness of the Gnostics for the first time. Jung was also a person who was haunted. His desire for personal authenticity and integration drove him to break with Freud and he emerged from this crisis with insights that are truly profound. At points Jung's haunting was quite literal, and his reception of the *Seven Sermons to the Dead* was accompanied by etheric and poltergeist activity:

> *The dead came back from Jerusalem, where they found not what they sought. They prayed me let them in and besought my word, and thus I began my teaching.*
> **Sermon 1, 1913.**

For more insight on this critical chapter of modern Gnostic history, you may want to check out Stephan Hoeller's excellent *The Gnostic Jung*.

In many ways my fairly persistent preoccupation with the Gnostics and heretical Christians is also evidence of my own ongoing wrestle with the ghost of Jesus past. This is a relationship that feels markedly different to previous attempts at belief and certainty, for now my haunting is about the discovery of what the sacred flame of my own Christhood might mean for my liberation.

Surreal Christology (Part 2): The Mirror

It's hardly surprising that mirrors get used a lot in magic; assuredly they are a bit weird. When we look at them they extend space, they reverse, and they potentially distort. Whatever we think we look like in our heads, when we look into a mirror we are pushed into a dialogue between our internalized self-perception and the version of self represented in front of us. We may be delighted by what we see or we may become flooded by dysmorphia. Our dis-ease may be skin deep, or it may reveal deeper truths about who we want to be and how we wish to interact with the world around us. Whatever we think is driving us, if we see ourselves more fully we may be confronted by aspects of our daemon that are as likely to shock as they are to empower.

The magical use of mirrors can be manifold, ranging from aids for spirit evocation to scrying tools that allow the diviner greater access to their own unconscious processes. To explore a mirror nocturnally, via candle-light, is to journey to occult edges, and the practice of covering mirrors following a recent death alludes to a need to stabilize our environment in the midst of grief. Given the way they seem to play with the nature of time and space, it's of little surprise that the Surrealists found them so fascinating.

The Surrealists on occasion had mirrors explicitly within their art (e.g., as puddles of quicksilver or mirrored melting clock faces) but more often their presence seems far more implicit. Via their use of depth of field and inversion, when we engage with surrealist art we can feel that we are gazing at a reflection, with all the subtle strangeness innate to that process. Like the melting clock, we are required to relinquish a hold on our sense of time and solidity; things get a bit wobbly and dream-like.

In many ways myth and mythic heroes can act as powerful mirrors for viewing ourselves. When we consider those stories or figures that we are drawn to, they can reveal some significant aspects of who we are at both a conscious and unconscious level. While our initial attraction to a myth may reflect a need or a connection that seems quite obvious e.g. a promise of liberation or an exemplar of individuation, when we renew and revisit this process over time, arguably something subtler takes place. When we truly engage with and internalize these spirits, their strangeness starts to haunt and shape our dreams and outlook.

In terms of my own experience, while my initial flight into Christianity was largely related to my adolescent confusion about the fluidity of my sexuality and gender identity, the Queerness of mystery still managed to break through via my interactions with the myth of Christ. While recognizing my personal projections onto the gospel narrative, I eventually uncovered in my reading of Jesus a blurry ambiguity that remains inspiring. Yes, this was still the radical who threw over tables in the temple, but he was also the mother hen who wanted to gather the lost beneath his wings.

In a personal world where the versions of maleness, certainty and force made little sense to me, my own gnostic encounter allowed access to a gentler, more mysterious experience. This

Surreal Christology (Part 2):
The Mirror

Christ became a mirror through which I could view myself more closely. Such looking can be far from comfortable, but over time it allowed me to engage with deeper truths about who I needed to become. This magical process of engaging with the Christ myth allowed me (somewhat ironically) to become accepting enough of myself that I no longer wished to call myself a Christian.

This Gnostic Christ seems to be asking me to take more responsibility for my path, while at the same time doing less violence to the core of who I am. This reflective process is most definitely a work-in-progress and has been far from tidy or pain-free. To walk a magical path requires that we "dare", even when it means the willed deconstruction of those stories and heroes we hold as precious. This is a narrow road, but it holds the potential of liberty from the claustrophobia of childlike sentimentality.

Whichever mythic mirror feels most attractive to you, I would recommend revisiting it with a Zen-like state of beginner's mind. Find some great art concerning these myths, or better yet create some art of your own. Often these creative explorations into the surreal and less lateral aspects of ourselves provide us with gateways to discovery and the possibility of further evolution.

Find art that feeds your soul and allows greater insight into who you are and who you can become. Use such art as the fuel to fire your journey in seeking the Mysteries!

Surreal Christology (Part 3): The Trickster

I'll be honest, part of problem with Tricksters is that the process of trying to define them can, in and of itself, be a bit tricky! The very nature of these liminal figures that push irreverently against what is polite, acceptable and knowable means that they tend to slip out of attempts at neat archetypal categorization. As with my previous explorations of Queer theory and the way in which its blurry fluidity can be liberating as well as infuriating, so attempts to corral figures as diverse as Hermes, Loki, Coyote and Eshu will almost certainly meet with frustration.

Tricksters tend to be those figures who dwell on the outer-edges of ordered society and who speak difficult truths regarding that culture's need to change and evolve. By inhabiting this prophetic, questioning role they are frequently seen as subversive agents of chaos seeking to destabilize the rule of law. While this may well be part of their role, like the heretic's relationship with more orthodox beliefs, the relationship between the Trickster and those in authority is often far more complex and symbiotic.

In many senses the depiction of Christ in both the canonical and Gnostic gospels can be seen as having a trickster-like role. Jesus spends time with sex workers and the drug dependent; he questions religious authority and seeks to challenge the servant/master paradigm of how we engage with the divine:

The kingdom of God is within you.

Gospel of Thomas, Saying 3

I no longer call you servants, because a servant does not know his master's business. Instead, I have called you friends.

John 15:15

Here we have Jesus as a prophet and reformer within the context of 1st century Palestine, challenging and questioning received orthodoxies. He asks his listeners to dig deeper, not as a rejection of historic teachings, but as a means of encountering a richer experience of truth:

Do not think that I have come to abolish the Law or the Prophets; I have not come to abolish them but to fulfil them.

Matthew 5:17

The disruptive anarchy of the Trickster can become a powerful catalysing agent that shifts perception and allows social evolution. This is rarely as smooth or as bloodless as it sounds, especially when acting prophetically challenges the excesses of hierarchy and control. Arguably the tipping point for Jesus in the gospel narratives was less about declaring the incoming of God's Kingdom and more about his denunciation of the misuse of religious power (Matthew 23). For the Trickster to speak truth to power is far from risk free and while Jesus' death was at least partially triggered by his own messianic self-perception, we may want to reduce such risks by being "as cunning as serpents" in determining how we deploy our insights.

Surreal Christology (Part 3):
The Trickster

Loki's flight to Jötunheim, WG Collingwood (1908)

Part of the Trickster's more general role within myth and culture seems to be about challenging our certainty about perception and what we think we know as real. I would suggest that this willingness to slip sideways into a blurrier, half-glimpsed reality is central to the work of both the magician and artist. To take the mantle of either of these roles is to imbibe the spirit of the Trickster and to work with the challenge that this can provide to your sense of self, and your relationships with those around you. To walk these paths skilfully usually entails profound degrees of work on the self at a conscious and unconscious level.

For the Surrealists, the Trickster was often present in portraiture, with the artist's depiction of self or others reflecting the incoming of new insight. The weird process of alchemy at work in surreal art makes vivid the way in which we try to make sense of mystery at a macrocosmic level and in relation to the differing aspects of ourselves. Our encounters with aspects of reality that are strange, bizarre or "dark" often shake us from automaton sleep-states. For the Gnostic explorer this is the still small voice of the Trickster that at once draws us in and disturbs us, causing us to question what we think we know so as to trigger new states of awakening. Unsurprisingly, Trickster gods like Eshu are the guardians of the crossroads and it is at these junctures of choice and liminality that we benefit most from their less lateral approach.

Whether via art, ritual theatre or an active engagement with our dreamscapes, those less-tidy, potentially disruptive aspects will demand that we give them space. To endlessly suppress or ignore them is to invite an eventual tsunami of shadow material that inevitably leads to widespread persecution of others onto whom our fears get projected. In my opinion, an acknowledgement of the Trickster and the creative power of misrule can be vital in fuelling and inspiring the changes we wish to see. While we must remain wary of the excesses of self-indulgence, embracing the Trickster can help us avoid the type of grim activism that loses sight of the happiness and peace that should hopefully accompany the freedom which we are pursuing.

Surreal Christology (Part 4): The Androgyne

Part of what appeals to me about Surrealism, as an artistic school and also as a way of engaging with human experience, is the way in which it seeks to embrace experiences of fluidity and uncertainty. Surrealist art dives deep into rich realms of the unconscious where attempts at neat categorization quickly start coming apart at the seams. This is a twilight realm in which polarities such as animal versus human, safety versus threat and male versus female are challenged and played with.

I have previously written about the way in which Queer theory and experience has provided me with a language for understanding the blurry liminality that I experienced in relation to my sexuality and in my spiritual explorations. Queer theory often provides an irreverent take on the complex interplay between biological sex and the way in which we perform our genders. This playfulness is as likely to be found in visual art as it is in text and depictions of Androgyny (religious and secular) can help us gain insight into this strange territory.

In the work of both Frida Kahlo and Leonora Carrington we can see that these female artists engage with depictions of the gendered body in ways which seek to disrupt many of the cultural expectations of their time. In Kahlo's work they powerfully utilized the juxtaposition of Mexican traditional dress with glorious facial hair as a means of representing a more authentic version of themselves. In both her art and life Kahlo bravely explored the fluidity of her gender presentation and bisexuality, despite her physical disabilities (resulting from childhood polio, and a traffic accident at the age of 18), and the personal turmoil she experienced. She even refused to be pigeon-holed as a Surrealist stating; "I never painted dreams. I painted my reality". In my view, artists such as Carrington and Kahlo worked with androgyny in a manner that embraced the dynamic and shifting nature of what this concept might mean. As Erin Hinz has observed in assessing themes of androgyny within Carrington's work:

Carrington experienced the social limits of her female body and choose to create bodies that fused these restrictive codes with animals, ancient ideologies in an alchemical way that transmuted these base constructions into precious, mystical and complex expressions of identity.

While the interplay of male and female aspects of the self was lauded in the works of Jung and by first-wave feminists (cf. Virginia Woolf's iconic *Orlando*) others have been less than keen. While the call of these early writers was taken up by later luminaries such as June Singer and Carolyn Heilbrun, some second-wave Feminist theologians such as Mary Daly saw it as an escapist trap that "sucks spellbound victims into itself". From the perspective of her radical separatism, Daly viewed it as an attack on the essential potency of womanhood ("Why do I need to be half-male?") and as an attempt to falsely reify certain qualities of humanity as being polarized "male" or "female". From such a perspective, the aspiration towards androgyny amounts to a form of sexual sublimation and fantasy that distances women from the visceral experience of female embodiment and passion.

While such voices need to be part of dialogue concerning androgyny, it could be argued that while they are seeking to challenge ideas of stereotyping and gendered fixity, via their biological essentialism they may be in danger of another existential cul de sac. While concepts of androgyny may well be in danger of minimizing difference and disregarding a true valuing of women's experience, the desire for such an essential separateness also risks missing experiences of playfulness and exploration that seem vital to shared human experience.

For me the challenging deconstruction offered by third-wave feminisms and Queer theory, is less about the removal of category and difference and more about a willingness to dance and blur at the edges of where we think such borders lie. There seems to be a psychological complexity to such approaches that allows for the power of dreams and the unconscious in allowing the primacy of the experimental and experiential. Perhaps we are back with the Trickster in prophetically destabilizing neat categorization and asking for the space to be uncertain and to explore.

It could be argued that much previous use of Androgyny as an aspiration and organizing principle has been based on a rather idealized dialectical process that actively seeks to smooth out potential tensions and the ragged edges of difference. In following good dialectical theory, apparently opposing positions (thesis and antithesis) are balanced and synthesized in order to produce a new, balancing, third position. In contrast to dialectics, a more dialogical approach seeks to enable differing positions and voices to sit alongside each other and maintain a multiplicity rather than needing to necessarily pursue compromise. This type of dialogical multiplicity holds a more Queered potential in allowing wider diversity and the potential of greater fluidity between positions. Dialectics certainly look neater on paper, but I would wonder about the extent to which they truly capture the messier (but potentially more interesting) terrain of our lives.

Y?

Surreal Christology (Part 4): The Androgyne

This queered vision of androgyny provides a sigil for challenging and shifting our sense of what we think we think we know. This androgynous mystery acts a mirror via which deeper aspects of self might be gleaned. Whether when gazing at our own reflection or seeing aspects of self in others, the presence of such oscillating fluidity can provide the possibility of change, and with change, hope.

In relation to my own journey I have sought to describe how my initial flight into Christianity was largely related to my adolescent confusion about the fluidity of my own sexuality and gender identity. Despite the damaging efforts of my self-suppression, I experienced at least a part of my liberation via my encounter with the Queer androgyny of Christ.

While owning my own needs and bias, I eventually encountered in my reading of Jesus a blurry ambiguity that provided me with an alternative mode of being. This was a Jesus who was able to direct his anger toward righteous ends, but also who blessed the gentle and sought out the one lost sheep. At a more cosmic level he was also the mythic Christ of the Gnostics, who as the "first Adam" existed in some spacey realm which at once contained many genders while being also beyond them. This metaphysical fluidity, whilst looking decidedly freaky to my fellow seminarians, provided me with a doorway through which I could begin a new chapter of greater self-understanding.

While the adherents of orthodox belief might seek the security of creedal statements in order to curtail their anxiety, the spiritual free-thinker in me takes a somewhat perverse pleasure trying to hold together a more complex picture with all the seeming contradictions that this entails. The dialogics of such a position create a type of dynamic friction and internal resistance that, when worked with consciously, can generate change.

Collage, Magic and the Unconscious

Whichever media the Surrealists worked in (painting, poetry, drawing) one of the consistent themes that runs throughout the School is their desire to work more overtly with the unconscious aspects of self. We have already considered the prevalence of dreams and dream-like states in the work of occult inspired artists such as Ernst and Carrington, and the way that their work used the juxtaposition of strange, jarring images as a way of articulating pre-verbal themes that emerge from the deepest dimensions of being.

The Surrealists were renowned for their inventiveness in developing a vast range of artistic techniques and strategies for seeking access to the creative dimensions of the unconscious self. This involved everything from relief rubbings ("frottage"), automatic painting, the creation of dream résumés and the artistic use of old parlour games such as Exquisite Corpse. One of the techniques that the Surrealists utilized to great effect was that of collage.

Collage (from the French *coller*, "to glue") is a technique of assemblage in which the artist brings together a number of different media and pulls them out of their original context in order to create a new reality in which radically different ideas and textures can overlap, contrast and interact in the eye of the viewer. Historically while example of collage can be found in 10th century Japan and in the Cathedrals of Medieval Europe, in relation to its use in Modern art, it is generally agreed that it was primarily developed in the works of Georges Braque and Pablo Picasso from 1912 onwards.

Max Ernst's artistic expression was hugely innovative. He is credited with the invention of the frottage technique and also made use of other approaches such as decalcomania (pressing paint between two surfaces). While Ernst worked in a wide range of media, his work with collage is especially inspiring. In works such as his surrealist novel *Une Semaine De Bonte: A Surrealist Novel in Collage* (1934), we witness his exploration of the jarring and animalistic dimensions of self. As Ernst himself observed regarding his absurd combinations of images, objects and text, they;

> *provoked a sudden intensification of the visionary faculties in me and brought forth an elusive succession of contradictory images ... piling up on each other with the persistence and rapidity which are peculiar to love memories and visions of half sleep.*

(Quoted in *Ernst* by Ian Turpin, p7)

Within his collage and his work more generally, Ernst repeatedly employs the symbol of the bird as a representation of himself. He named this avian manifestation of himself "Loplop", whom he saw as the "superior of the birds". When viewed through a more occult lens, I am struck by the potential parallels between these images and the concept of the Witch's familiar or the animal aspect of the self, referred to as the "fetch" in Norse soul lore. Via its window into the darker, unconscious aspects of self, collage provides a means through which strange and even macabre images can provide insight to our own process of self-understanding.

Exercise 2: The Witch's Collage

In assembling our Heretic's altar we sought to incorporate those images, ideas and icons that inspired our own process of spiritual freethinking. These subjects will now become even more helpful as we work with this exercise which uses collage as a means of delving into the surreal realm of our unconscious.

I will state at the outset that there are a myriad of ways of working magically with collage, and I offer this exercise as but one example (albeit a creative and tested one!) for intrepid explorers. Unlike their more randomized postmodern cousin, cut-ups, collages seek to work more deliberately with aspects of the unconscious from the outset of the artist's project of creation. Hopefully, having begun a process of reflection regarding your heretical inspirations as we begin this activity, the images, symbols and colour associations will begin to bubble to the surface.

To provide you with a bit of structure you might want to follow some of the following steps:

1. Find the images and symbols that you feel capture the essence of your journey into heretical freethinking. Don't be weighed down by the expectations of others! If cartoon heroes or industrial noise musicians do it for you, include them alongside more standard spiritual symbology.
2. Assemble art stuff. At a minimum you will need scissors, glue, pens and pencils. Coloured paper of differing textures works

and you may want to incorporate pieces of text. Your imagination is the only real limit here! Make sure you have a large piece of paper or card (A3 or bigger) so that you have enough space to stick your stuff onto.

3. Find a space that you feel comfortable in. Ideally you should be able to spread your images and materials out so that you can see the possible directions that your collage can take. Personally I like having some music on to inspire me and I usually need a minimum of 45 minutes to an hour to let the collage take shape. Having a time limit can be helpful for this specific exercise, in that it provides an end point rather than having to struggle with that sense of not knowing when you've done enough.

4. Like the approach of sleep, light hypnosis, and some meditative states, this work will be best approached with a sense of playfulness and a desire to not take it too seriously. Let your eyes move over your assembled materials and images and simply begin. You can't get this wrong; your images and textures will build naturally during the duration of the work.

5. Often our results can surprise us. What I love about collage is the way in which it can have various pockets of activity and interest. Our eyes may be drawn to one thematic cluster only to realize that there's something really interesting in another part of our work.

6. When our collage is completed, we can put it to any number of ritual uses. I usually place mine in the corner of the house

Collage, Magic and the Unconscious

where I meditate and do ritual work. This allows my attention to come back to it repeatedly and spot emerging themes.

7. Given the connection between collage, the unconscious and the realm of dreams, one interesting practice could involve placing your collage under your bed or pillow prior to sleep. Spend some time before sleep meditating on your collage and let the interplay of images and textures enhance your nocturnal journeying!

Playing with Queer Cut-ups

I'm sitting in the front room of a dear magical colleague (Julian Vayne) and I'm surrounded by a multitude of artefacts from past rituals, and hours spent in meditation. While the wood burner and main altar space provide a natural centrepiece, today my eyes are drawn to the array of cut-up collages that bedeck one of the walls. These are not elaborate or overly wrought attempts at occult art; rather they represent raw, psychic high-dives in order to explore fragments of self and the processes that unfold as we try to explore darker, stranger terrain.

Cut-up

Given the exploration of Queer identity that we have been undertaking together, I started reflecting on the possible connections between how cut-ups and Queer dynamics might interact in our process of exploring Self.

I have previously written on how cut-ups might interact with aspects of ego psychology, but in seeking to track the historic relationship between movements such as the Beats and the emergence of Queer identity, it got me to wondering further about how cut-ups might represent a highly queered and magical form of expression. As I observed back then:

> *Like collage, cut-ups seek to use existing material in new ways that often involve the combining and juxtaposition of words and images so as to create new insight and meaning.*
>
> *In tracking the lineage of cut-ups as an approach, from the surrealism of the Dadaists, Brion Gysin, Burroughs and Genesis P-Orridge, we can begin to see the depth of magical thinking embedded in this technique. As we seek to engage with and manipulate reality, the cut-up not only embodies the desired efficacy of our sorcery, but also the fluid shape-shifters that our arte forces us, the magician, to become. If our magic has any real depth, then our ego must undergo a similar process of reassembly.*

Chaos Craft

Cut-ups are a potent means of challenging our attempts at fixed certainty and polarity. Ideas and images that we previously kept apart are cast together in potentially abrupt disruption. These cut-ups don't allow for tidy answers or for a buttoned-up, linear sense of self, rather they represent a bubbling up from the unconscious that may reveal as much about the dynamic tensions

Playing with Queer Cut-ups

at work as they do potential answers. Apparently unconnected images are juxtaposed with stark headline text and so new meanings and connections are made. To me this dynamic process feels potentially unsettling and hugely creative.

The Queer self is one that has a profound connection to the constructed and performed. As an outsider position it has had to survive by being magpie-like in pulling together those jewels and glimmering half-truths that help make sense of what it means to live with a greater sense of magic and power. Others may dismiss its rag-tag approach for its lack of coherence, but like the trickster or the holy fool it holds up a mirror to those parts of culture whose attempts at control appear all too reliant on dusty outdated certainties.

Wild words

The playful complexity of Queer identity is one that disrupts my attempts at locating my sense of self in fixed descriptors and concrete identities. Any attempt to side-step curiosity and open-handed questioning is unlikely to withstand Queer's rainbow-laser side-eye. This type of awareness asks that we acquire and develop skills that allow us to more effectively tolerate process, journey and uncertainty.

Similarly, the process of the cut-up requires vulnerability as we step back, allowing patterns and (potential) meanings to emerge. Techniques such as cut-ups and automatic writing/drawing are certainly more towards the artistic end of the "Art and Science" dialectic, but such creativity shouldn't be mistaken for laxity. Ironically it often seems that as we seek to make use of approaches that are less linear and apparently chaotic, that we have to exercise a more focused sense of awareness in gaining benefit from them. It may be that those people who are drawn to more scripted workings do so because it provides them with a greater sense of security and control.

One of the primary reasons that I was drawn to the magical path was its sense of collaboration and play. Worldviews and metaphysics that declared absolute certainty were no longer viable, but I was still hungry to explore the mystery of consciousness and the glimpses of awakening that were coming in and out of view. Techniques like cut-ups and collage can provide us with potent and creative means for accessing new insights regarding the paths we are seeking to walk. They are rarely complete answers, more often they are snapshots of a work in progress that we may need to slow down and wait for, rather than rushing to a sensible, adult conclusion.

Exercise 3: Cut-ups

In contrast to the rather leisurely and reflective collage exercise, the cut-up is an expression of the chaotic and random and is injected with a large dose of punk rock energy. While I tend to take at least 45 minutes to assemble a collage (basically at least an album's listening time), this cut-up should take less than 10 minutes (one long house track or four punk tracks!).

Cut-ups have a randomized, almost divinatory feel to them. As with most divination, these techniques tend to produce a more interesting result when we have a clear question or issue in mind as we undertake them. The symbols, images and associated phrases that are part of whichever method we employ, interact with our question and our consciousness so as to provide new insight.

Given that our previous exercises (The Heretic's Altar and The Witch's Collage) have been focused on those sources of personal spiritual influence that inspire us in our pursuit of liberty, I propose that we use a cut-up working to further this process.

Purpose: To use a cut-up to provide insight into an aspect of my identity e.g. spiritual direction, career path, sexual identity etc.

Method:

1. Find a selection of magazines, newspapers, fast-food adverts etc. that you are happy to demolish in the process of the cut-up.
2. Find enough energizing music to fill up the 10 minutes of your working.
3. Assemble glue, scissors and source material along with a large piece of card or paper onto which the cut-up will be stuck.
4. Go! Start cutting up images and phrases that catch your eye. Abandon for now thoughts of coherence and the making of meaning. Just pull together those things that strike you. I generally find it best to stick them down as I'm going. While I'm undoubtedly shaping and creating meaning as I go, I still want to retain some of the randomized haphazard approach that is part of the spirit of cut-ups.
5. Stop! Once your music has finished, step away from your work and have a cup of tea (other less amazing beverages are available). Now, with tea in hand, revisit the scene of your working. As with our collage, when viewing our cut-up we try to let our consciousness slip sideways and adopt a type of less judgmental beginner's mind.
6. In this state of what Freud called "free floating intent", start to notice any connecting themes or synchronicities. Try not to worry if they seem strange or jarring. If you use a magical diary record what you've seen.
7. As with our collage, you can use this cut-up as a meditation guide or as a nocturnal trigger for shaping your dream life.

Great Questions, Great Answers

At the beginning of 2017 I took part in the excellent Occult Conference at Glastonbury where I had the good fortune to be co-presenting with Andrew Phillip Smith on "Gnosticism in Theory and Practice: Gnosticism as a path of spiritual Free-thinking". In pursuit of an engaging format, Andrew and I decided that we would pose to each other a series of questions about this theme in the hope that we could provide some interesting and erudite responses. I will leave the assessment of our success to the audience, but one of the most intriguing questions that Andrew asked was whether I had encountered any interesting spiritual beings during my gnostic explorations.

I have always been impressed by the clarity and thoughtfulness of Andrew's work, so it should have come as little surprise that his question triggered an interesting process of self-reflection and insight. In short, my most memorable experiences to date have been with Holy Wisdom (Sophia), and with my future magical self.

I have already written at some length in *A Gnostic's Progress* about my work with the figure of Sophia, and while I have engaged with a number of god-forms in my magical work, I have been struck by the depth of her impact on me. I had long been acquainted with the personification of Wisdom as female within biblical literature, but by engaging with her magically via Gnostic myth, I felt as though I have been given a new lens through which to view with the female divine across a number of intersecting traditions. Sophia has led me to deep waters of Bhakti (devotional) yoga that has allowed me to access a state of emotional openness that seems largely absent from much Western magical practice. I rarely feel comfortable talking about the deeply personal dimensions of my magical work, in that I find language often struggles to capture nuance without risking cliché, but I would encourage you, dear reader, to explore for yourself the connections between Wisdom and the divine feminine in whichever path you follow.

It is perhaps slightly comical that as a Gnostic explorer I continue to be shocked by the direct challenge that this work poses, but I guess we are all prone to forgetfulness. In exploring the process of my own waking up, I have been aware of my own spark of awareness being embodied by a figure dwelling at the threshold of my consciousness. In exploring together the powerful impact that Surrealism can have on our magical practice, I have already mentioned my sense of being haunted by the memory of the Jesus I had encountered during my Christian past, but this sense of unease has a different quality. Differing schools may seek to describe this mysterious figure as an etheric double or the daemonic aspect of the self, but my own encounter seemed quite strongly connected to my own future self. This sense of personified aspiration, or what Assagioli would call the Super-Conscious self, acted as a "dweller on the threshold" who seemed to be beckoning me ever forward. This figure has many resonances mythically, and aspects of them can be felt in figures such as the androgynous

Adam Kadmon from the Jewish tradition or Balder, "the shining one" from Norse lore. Whatever figure we may connect to, perhaps a more pressing issue is how we draw inspiration from them and connect to the sense of becoming or unfolding they represent.

Bright God

Working with such figures allows me to walk the path of aspiration, guarded futurism and teleological endeavour. Magical work that has no aspiration or no real longing that it is seeking to fulfil is unlikely to sustain focus. Most of us who seek to follow an initiatory or magical path do so because we want more. We aspire to understand our past and who we are today so that we might maximize our being, and pull in gnosis from our future magical selves.

Nema, in her excellent *Maat Magick*, locates such work in the figure of N'Aton, an androgynous future self that holds within it our individual and collective genius:

> *In N'Aton's home line (i.e. the version of the future in which they are most fully realized), we've controlled our mutation into a species of double consciousness: the familiar one of individuality and the new telepathic connection amongst us that constitutes N'Aton.*
>
> **Ma'at Magick, p65**

Personally I love this perception of awakening as holding both individual and collective dimensions. N'Aton represents a non-binary 'They' at a number of levels and this is represented by their imag—half in starry shadow and half in light, their gender is located in a third place that dances between and beyond polarities.

Each of us will have our own personal mission or unique challenge in seeking psychological integration; some will need to reach out to make more connections with others, while others will need to seek the isolate embodiment of consciousness as a way of establishing individual ego-strength. N'Aton reminds us that in the aeon of Ma'at, both must be held in her balancing scales.

Just Goddess

My own ongoing explorations of N'Aton as a concept/being feel fruitful, in that such workings can provide new insight regarding the real nature of what we are aspiring to be, and the challenges that might limit such becoming. Such work can be quite edgy and disorientating (time-travel often can be!) and I would recommend thorough grounding at the conclusion of your ritual working; banish, eat and preferably have contact with others.

The Heretic's Journey - Steve Dee

What follows is a brief snapshot from a recent invocation to N'Aton that took place as part of a ritual in our magical lodge that explored our hopes and longings from the future:

> N'Aton:
> Deep Self
> Future Self
> Quicksilver Messenger
> Who dwells on the Threshold.
> Genius!
> Daemon!
> Dark-Feather Wind-Dancer.
> Holy Guardian Angel,
> Speak to us and support us.
> Pull us forward
> Come dwell with us now!

Further Adventures in Ma'at Magick

While the primary structure of the book Ma'at Magick follows the time-tested format of the Hermetic Kabbalah, for me the juiciest insights are gained as Nema incorporates her more Typhonic and Nu-Thelemic inspirations. Having worked closely with Kenneth Grant and the Kaula Nath lineage of AMOOKOS, her work weaves together a wide variety of magical strands which become manifest in this book.

One of the areas of magical practice that seems to reflect this rich material is Nema's work with the Forgotten Ones. For her, these are the personified aspects of our ancient and primal drives that have allowed humanity to survive and evolve. These are the lurkers in the deep that connect us to the potent needs of hunger, sex, clan connection, communication and curiosity. As Nema observes: "Civilisation, law, governance and good manner form a fragile veneer over the survival urges in the human unconscious."

Once one has entered into conversation with the Holy Guardian Angel, Nema believes that it is vital to engage in our work with the Forbidden Ones so as to avoid the perils of megalomania and potential magical burn-out. For us to truly earth our experiences of transcendence and the sense of who we might become, it is essential that as magicians we remain connected to the earthy reality of who we are as human animals. For our work to have sustainability, the balancing scales of Ma'at need to be attended to. If we focus only on the future, the "spiritual" and the new, we risk fragility and escapism. If we focus only on the ancestral drives of the past, we risk getting bogged down in materialism and missing the possibility of who we might become. Like the scales we seek balance, a Hermetic tightrope walk of "as above so below".

Part of the genius of author-artists such as Nema, Kenneth Grant and Austin Osman Spare is their appreciation of the 'darker', dream-like dimensions of magical work and how critical these are in fuelling a more integrated version of magical advancement. While critics might depict such approaches as being 'nightside', I couldn't frankly care less as my own experience with dusty, linear approaches is that they often fill the head while doing little for the heart or the body. For our alchemy to be real we need the fuel of body, mind and emotions ignited and transformed.

This need to reconnect to the Forgotten, dark and unconscious has been a theme key to my own magical journey. The psychological struggle to hide aspects of myself behind a mask of perceived respectability drove me down into what felt like a pit of confusion and personal torment. While I longed for a quick fix that demanded less effort or a ready rescuer, the answer came via darkness, stillness and the eventual death of who I thought I was. While these days I find limited value in terms such as 'Left-hand path', I can still recognize the territory it is attempting to map in trying to describe those spiritual paths that engage with the dark, earthy and potentially frightening dimensions of existence.

In revisiting these insights of Nema's, I was reminded of my own ongoing focus on the form of draconian magic as articulated in the works of Michael Kelly. In works such as *Apophis* and *Aegishjalmur*, Kelly describes the work of the initiate as being an ongoing dialogue between consciousness and chaos. Yes, we might strive for an awakened sense of self that seeks the qualities of Godhood, but we must also recognize the darker more chaotic currents of the Serpent moving through the depths of ourselves and the cosmos. The true adept is the one able to acknowledge the presence of chaos and order within their personal sphere, and understand that both impulses can be harnessed when done so consciously.

While the approaches outlined by Nema and Kelly might differ significantly in their chosen starting point and aesthetics, their shared authenticity is found in their balancing of a wide range of human needs and competing drives. Our personal journeys and tastes will of course shape the degree of comfort and congruence with any given path, but my hunch is that any school or method of lasting value will force us to confront those forgotten aspects that potentially hold the key to deeper progress.

Working with Recent Ancestors

In my explorations of the Ma'at current, I have once again been struck by the importance of how we work with concepts of balance and time within the magical project of personal and collective alchemy. As already considered, I believe that part of the genius of Nema's work is the way in which the scales of Ma'at seek balance in the present by consciously engaging with the future (as embodied by N'Aton), and the history of our primal drives (the Forgotten Ones).

The moment of Truth

As part of my day-job I run a small family therapy clinic that aims to help groups of people consider how they communicate with each other. When I sit with families of all different shapes and sizes (some formed by biology and others by intention), I try to invite them to be curious about how they connect to each other and also whether there are ways in which they would like to improve communication. Part of what we do together is to adopt a detective-like interest in the unspoken principles that shape our interactions. When these principles are applied to the practicalities of daily life they can become manifested as 'scripts' that determine the way people relate to each other. As with scripts in a play, we are often given rules about a whole range of things (such as who cooks the food and who resolves the arguments) that have been handed to us by previous generations. These scripts are frequently shaped by deep-seated beliefs regarding gender, illness and success, and within families we can be warned against departure from these via cautionary family legends regarding disasters that will befall us if we do.

In exploring with people why they think this type of therapy might help, our initial piece of work is regularly focused on trying to bring these previously buried beliefs above ground. One tool that we can employ to unearth this material is a genogram, or family tree. By mapping out the members of a family through three or four generations, we can begin to gain a picture of how styles and stories have been co-created over time. The scripts we inherit aren't necessarily a bad thing, but the people who attend family therapy are doing so because these scripts are no longer functional and are causing people to get stuck.

This is a process of externalization where (at least for that moment) we consciously consider a difficulty as if it were separate from the group or individual reflecting upon them. When we can name the scripts at work and the principles that might lay behind them, so we can create a small sense of space within which they might be explored. In being able to stand slightly meta to these narratives, we can begin to consider the possibility of improvising new styles of interaction that allow different types of behaviour to be considered.

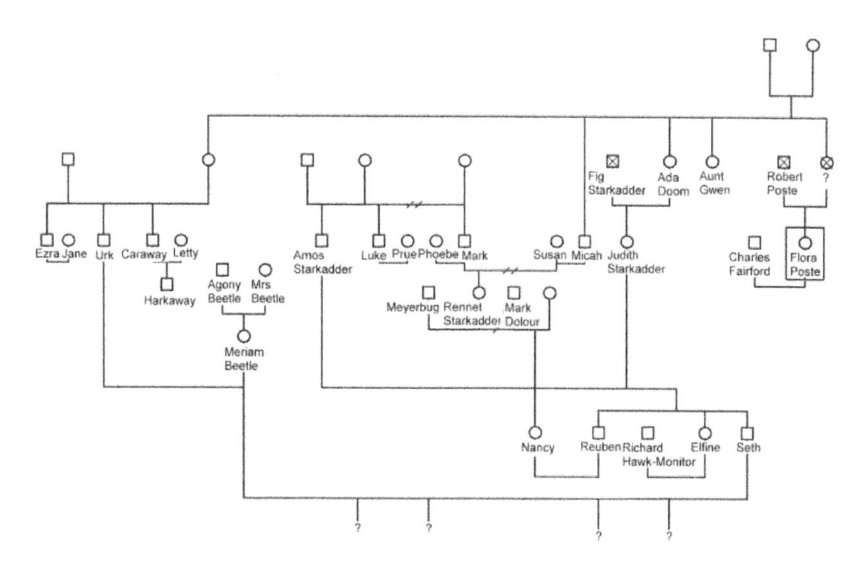

Genogram, or Sigil; or both?

As you are reading my description of this style of work, I'm hoping that you, as magically curious folks, are beginning to spot parallels with some of the ritual processes that you are engaged in. Magic that has a focus on the initiatory transformation of Self almost inevitably has to engage with some of the baggage and conditioning that we have inherited. If my magic is focused on allowing more liberated and peaceful versions of who I am, then I will need to begin a process on naming those inherited scripts/thoughtforms/entities that I experience as limiting. Whether we describe this conditioning in terms of Tantric Kleshas (shells) that need breaking down, or as parasitic entities that need to be ritually contained, by magically externalizing them, we create the possibility of engaging with them in a more creative manner.

This process of trying to understand repeating patterns of behaviour and how they have been manifested within an individual's history has also been helpful in my own work with my ancestors. At the beginning of our monthly Zen Hearth we consciously honour "Our Gods, Our Ancestors and the Spirits of this Place" and like many people not every ancestral relationship is an easy one. Being able to take one step back in trying to understand the origins of difficult dynamics has allowed me to gain some insight on any positive values they have passed to me. This does not absolve anyone of abusive behaviour, but it does provide a potential opportunity for gaining a new and wider perspective.

For me the therapy room and the magical circle have a number of similarities. Hopefully each provides the opportunity for safe exploration, the gaining of insight and the potential for healing. These environments invite us to take risks, but with any luck the scaffolding of solid theory and good practice allow us some degree of confidence in stepping out. In my experience, both work well when there is a high level of transparency about the process being undertaken and sensitivity to the dynamics of power at play.

Part of why I continue to describe myself as being a magician as well as being a bit of a mystic, is that in contrast to some forms of mystical encounter, I work hard at naming and understanding the process of what I do. Yes emotional and/or mystical stuff may occur as a result of my framing of my ritual activity, but the scene setting and conscious structure of the work allows me a more conscious process of integration. I have lots of builders and crafts people in my family line, and although many of them might struggle with the strange path I have followed, I hope that at least they can appreciate my attention to detail!

Ma'at, Typhonic Strands and AMOOKOS

In the course of seeking to deepen my own work with the Ma'at current, I have engaged in a reflection upon how these ideas of balance and integration have been central to my own pursuit of magical work. Alongside my exploration of Chaos Magic, probably the other, most informative contribution has come from the East/West tantric tradition of AMOOKOS. What follows is far from definitive, but hopefully allows for further reflection and an appreciation of the unique contribution that the AMOOKOS (Arcane and Magickal Order Of the Knights Of Shambhala) current has made to the current magical revival.

In considering my own magical development, and the role that the AMOOKOS work has had in shaping my evolution, I was struck by some of the often unspoken commonalities that seem to be shared between some of the main practitioners within the tradition. When assessing the contribution and histories of those adepts whose work I have come to respect, I have been struck by the significant influence of what we might broadly describe as the Typhonian tradition.

While we may gain much from an in-depth discussion as to what we mean by the descriptor 'Typhonian', for the purposes of this reflection I am using it to broadly categorize those people who have been shaped significantly by the work, ideas and writing of

Kenneth Grant. As I hope will become clear, the people who have been involved with the AMOOKOS work have each taken his inspirational work in unique and interesting directions, whilst having a shared appreciation of the spiritual terrain he was seeking to map.

Mike writes: "This picture is of Kenneth and me in 1978 in our flat in Golders Green, just round the corner from where he lived. I am missing him. He was a master of wisdom. I venerate his memory." Kenneth Grant and Mike Magee, photo by Jan Magee by kind permission.

The genesis of AMOOKOS is often considered to be the result of Mike Magee's (Sri Lokanath) initiatory relationship with Sri Mahendranath (Dadaji) and the seismic impact that this had on

Ma'at, Typhonic Strands and AMOOKOS

his personal magical universe. While the encounter with Dadaji was undoubtedly powerful in setting Mike along a path via which he came to be recognized as an expert Sanskrit scholar and translator of key Tantric texts, I have wondered whether the richness of the AMOOKOS current is derived from a more complex interplay.

Prior to this shift Mike had worked for some seven years with Kenneth Grant and while he was clear on the profound change wrought by contact with Dadaji, it would be fair to speculate as to the degree that his earlier work with Grant continued to be foundational. We know from Grant's history (as depicted within *At the Feet of the Guru*) that he himself had had direct contact with Yogic teaching and technique, and Mike is quite open about how the presence of this material in his work with Grant catalysed his own journey eastwards. Prior to travelling to India and encountering Dadaji, Mike had already begun mantra work, embarked on in-depth studies of Sidereal astrology and Sanskrit, and was familiar with Kashmir Shaivism. While the work with Grant was undoubtedly rich and challenging, he was unable to offer Mike the type of direct initiatory experience he was seeking in order to affirm the knowledge he had gained.

Far be it from me to make comment on the internal dynamics of a Guru-Chela relationship and the whole complex of relationships and community politics that resulted from Sri Lokanath's work with Dadaji. As some may know, much ink has been spilt and opinion expressed as to how Dadaji's declining health impacted on his relationships with those close to him. What I feel to be worthwhile is to describe my own sense of why I and others continue to experience the idea and curriculum of AMOOKOS as having spiritual value.

Having spent significant parts of my adolescence exploring the spiritual traditions of Buddhism and Hinduism, when I began training as a magician in my mid-20s, the East-West synthesis that I experienced in the AMOOKOS work made a great deal of sense to me. Here was a magical group that made use of Yogic technique and perspectives while at the same time incorporating the liberty and self-determination associated with the philosophy of Thelema.

My own route into the AMOOKOS work was via the writing and inspiration of Mogg Morgan. I was fortunate to receive some mentoring from Mogg over a number of years and was eventually given diksha by him. Mogg's work with the Egyptian God Set is well known and he is quite open about the early impact that his time in Kenneth Grant's Typhonian Order (the then *Typhonian Ordo Templi Orientis*, TOTO) had on his magical development.

Having made some links with Mogg via the Oxford Golden Dawn Society, I dug into his Tankhem writings that sought to draw parallels between the God Set and the path of Tantra. What could the recovery of the myth of this "Hidden God" reveal about the diversity of the Egyptian tradition; and how might Tantric and early Hermetic traditions cross-fertilize? This is heady territory, and part of my own desire for closer links with AMOOKOS were significantly influenced by Mogg's interest in the early history of these Typhon-Tantra links.

As I dove into the AMOOKOS grade papers (initially published as *Tantra Magick*) I was struck by the helpful way in which Mike sought to lead the aspirant through a process of self-understanding that would allow for the cultivation of Svvechacharya (true Will). The path of Tantra is often described as that of the Virya, or hero, and when expressed within the tribe of practitioners of the Nath sampradya, the Thelemic goal of awakening and self-sovereignty seemed especially to the fore.

Kalachakra thangka painted in Sera Monastery, Tibet.

In my experience, the beauty of Tantra Magic as a curriculum is that rather than being left with a vague sense that we should pursue "Peace, Freedom and Happiness", we are given some clear exercises to help us in developing a more Tantric appreciation of our lives. Time does not allow a full exposition here, but Sri Lokanath does a masterful job in exploring themes as wide ranging as the awakening of the senses, the nature of time, and the conscious use of the persona in interacting with the world. Mike does a gallant job in wrestling with the Tantric project of engaging with the realm of the body and life's earthiness as a means of awakening, and seeking to answer the question of what it might mean to become more fully human.

The heydays of AMOOKOS in the early 1980s provided inspiration and direction for innovative magicians on both sides of the Atlantic. Not only do we have the emergence of Chaos Magic (again heavily influenced by Grant), but we also have the Voudon-Gnostic research of Michael Bertiaux (see *Cults of the Shadow*) and the Post-Satanic work of Michael Aquino as manifest in the Temple of Set. For me personally, one key figure to emerge from this occult maelstrom was Maggie Ingalls.

Known more commonly as Nema, Ingalls worked directly with Grant within the TOTO, and her inspired engagement with Frater Achad's work with the Aeon of Maat is described in some detail by Grant in *Outside the Circles of Time*. Via her work with Maat, Nema received a channelled work via an androgynous figure from the future that she identified as N'Aton. For her, the Aeons of Horus and Maat formed a complementary whole or "double current", with the scales of Maat providing a feminine counter-balance to the surging energy of the conquering child. In addition to working with a collective of ritual magicians in the Cincinnati area, Nema was also an initiate within the AMOOKOS tradition. While I am unfamiliar with many of the adepts working at this time, figures such as Denny Sargent (Hermeticusnath) and Jan Fries were also instrumental in articulating a fusion of Typhonian, Maatian and Nath-Tantric currents.

I hope what this potted history is helping to illustrate is that there seems to be lots of thoughtful, creative magicians finding inspiration from the Yogic approach of AMOOKOS and the potent, nightside explorations of the Typhonian current. While this is an interesting intersect to note, perhaps the more pressing (and potentially inspiring) question is why these approaches are experienced as being complimentary?

Like his teacher Crowley, Grant's genius is arguably that he was at once a great innovator and a great assimilator of other sources. In his desire to explore mystery, Grant engaged with a broad range of occult practitioners (Crowley, Spare, Bertiaux and Nema) and filtered their insights through his own magical imagination. In considering the commonalities between the luminaries that inspired him, I am struck by their shared engagement with the unconscious and their use of visual art as a means of accessing it.

Grant's magical exploration of dark Stygian depths and weird stellar realms seem to embody a more Lunar-Vaginal Thelema in contrast to Crowley's Solar-Phallic one. We are grappling here with binaries and the dangers of over-simplification, but it does feel that Crowley's somewhat outdated, linear Victoriana was counter-balanced brilliantly by Grant's strange, writhing surrealism.

This is where the strength of something like the AMOOKOS work comes into its own. While Kenneth Grant's work is strong in the evocation of mood and sense of how strange the magical universe can be, arguably he is weaker at communicating what precisely one does (in terms of technique) to actually get to it, and remain there.

If Crowley (and Parsons) introduced us to the way in which the pursuit of Babalon can fuel our personal Grail quest, then Grant confronts us with the disturbing cost that the pursuit of Shakti might entail. If we seek an experience of the Goddess that moves beyond two-dimensional wish-fulfillment, then it is likely that we will need to make contact with those sources that have evolved a deeper appreciation. It feels likely to me that part of the attraction to Tantra for second and third generation Thelemites is the way in which it offers richer, time-tested means for experiencing She who births, loves and destroys.

Balance is always difficult to maintain, both in terms of our own personal equilibrium and in addressing the various domains of magical development within the context of an Order. Active skills versus cultivating receptivity, prescription versus personal liberty, and group versus solo practice are all competing needs that we seek to balance in ensuring a holism to our learning. In my experience curriculums such *Liber MMM* and *Tantra Magick* tend to have an enduring value in that they provide substance and suggestion without demanding adherence to material that may not fit too well with individual disposition. As Mike himself states in *Tantra Magick*:

> *This expression of the I Ching reveals the dynamic magick of AMOOKOS. The Ridgepole is the fluid yet equipoised point existing between the two states of active/passive.*
>
> **Tantra Magick, p93.**

Having waxed lyrical for over 1,500 words about the benefits that working with this curriculum offers those wanting a deeper experience of the Thelemic and Typhonian currents, one may rightly wonder, "Well, why isn't AMOOKOS that functional as an Order anymore?" The answer to this question is complex in that it is connected to the question of whether we believe formal magical Orders remain valuable; and also, which measure we use in quantifying success.

While formal Orders may have a specific and valuable role in the early stages of a person's magical development, I would wonder whether longer term involvement is essential as a universal aspiration. Social media and a greater espousal of "Open Source" philosophy, mean that for many there is far easier access these days to arcane information and the possibility of discussing its meaning with others. While I still personally believe that there is much to gain from experiencing the demands and checks that Orders can provide, I am also aware that much energy can be expended in political struggles and in perpetuating ideas that while once helpful are now largely irrelevant.

Many of those people who were members of Grant's TOTO report the rather strange experience of having made progress and then being kicked out. Now while on one level this might appear a bit odd, it may be an initiatory masterstroke! If we reflect upon the way in which a variety of adepts have taken their initial inspiring experience of the Typhonian current and then dispersed it more widely into occult culture, then we might choose to adopt poetic images about dandelions having succeeded at the point when they manage to disperse their seed to the wind.

In many ways I see the current role of AMOOKOS as being quite similar to this. As a functional Order that convenes lots of lively gatherings it's frankly a bit of a failure (at least currently in the UK). What I do think it succeeds in doing is in providing a node of practice, thought and inspiration around how we integrate Yogic thinking with Thelemic philosophy in its broadest sense. It is my hope that it can still offer some supportive mentoring and friendship to those wanting to evolve a more balanced Magical path in which solar, lunar, light and shadow are allowed to dance together. By seeking to make transparent the ongoing influence of the Typhonian tradition on its form of Tantra, it is my hope that we can move beyond over-dependence on idealized teachers, or the pursuit of a style of Hindu re-enactment that fails to bring us closer to greater freedom. As Mike wisely observes in the introduction to *Tantra Magic*:

If the work of the Amookos grades was successful, an individual would finally realise that the grades and work were simply a means to an end, to be discarded once the essence was extracted. ... Names such as Nath, and groups such as Amookos, could only remain as relative things. When spirit is free, what matter the name its outer form is given?

Many thanks to Mike Magee and Mogg Morgan for giving this piece the once-over and filling in some historical gaps.

An Audience with Charlotte Rodgers

Charlotte Rodgers is a writer, artist and magical person. In thinking further about how the processes of Art and Magic inform each other, I asked for an interview, and she kindly agreed to discuss how these interact within her work.

SD: Could you tell us a little about your own magical background? (How you got into it.)

CR: I don't think one's intrinsic being changes much from early childhood, aside from layering up a load of behavioural baggage and experiences to obscure, and hopefully at times to enhance, our essential self. I always had a spiritual world view, highlighted by a personality that had a great deal of difficulty relating to others. At times, I lived with my grandmother where I was overexposed to fundamentalist Catholicism which I found fascinating; but I found the premise of good and evil made no sense to me (I was a precocious child... and looking back perhaps a bit ADD or sociopathic). As a child, I was obsessed with books, my microscope, astronomy, archaeology and mythology; constantly looking for other worlds that I could relate to as this one made no sense!

I was seven or so when I came across *Man, Myth and Magic* and it was like boom bang... this was IT!

I used to see colours and shapes and always believed in magic. I remember being about 10 and walking home from the cinema with my little sister and telling her, 'I'm a witch, watch... the lights at every crossing we come to will turn green when we approach them'... there were about seven I think on our walk home and indeed each one did turn green.

By age 12 I was into tarot and palmistry and started studying various magickal practices consciously. I also later studied Phenomenology of Religion for O-levels and A-levels and simply enough, was always searching for something.

As with inherent approaches to learning that tailor for individuals through hearing, seeing or experiencing, people have different ways of understanding their reality. Philosophical (relating to ideas) political (relating to structures) and spiritual (relating to 'other'). A bit simplistic perhaps but it makes sense to me, and my frame for experience and perception is very much a spiritual one.

So, I've always been magical, and constantly been trying to understand and work with this, whilst trying to sort my life out on a mundane level.

You've worked in a few different traditions, could you tell us about those and which approaches you currently find most meaningful?

My answer for this is a continuation from the above in many ways. I'm not a group person in that I cannot cope with the structures and power plays that often deviate (some may say develop) a tradition and cause it to lose its original premise.

The Hermit by Charlotte Rodgers

Conversely, I love the inspirational buzz and play I get from working with a group. For a long time, there was a sense of 'should do' or 'should be' in my practice. I 'should' develop discipline in my practice by adhering to a certain tradition and following its rules, I 'should' validate myself by reading certain books or following the rules, though my essential magical self just loves to play and when I'm working with the right current, it's a flow, a key to a lock.

I'm also no good with names and that is a big problem with some traditions... I just can't get my head around identification of energies with certain titles... works in my head but my magickal self just wants to toss it all aside.

I immersed myself in Crowley's teachings for many years. It was accessible at the time and very interesting. Parts of them I found very workable and at that time I felt that as a woman it gave me more validity than accepting more nature related witchcraft which came so naturally to me living in New Zealand and later in Asia. I was a member of a few groups, and seemed to work well with certain currents that though I didn't relate to a specific named god or spirit form, say Set, I could relate to their essence and work incredibly well with them. Later I was initiated into the Uttara Kaula and AMOOKOS which also made sense to me on many levels but I reached a point of self-confidence where I started stripping back, and realizing that my magic was an intuitive path, and I was trying to follow the rules of others, a method which had become counterproductive.

Some of the traditions that resonate for me, such as Haitian Voodoo or Santeria I've learned from and respect but take no further. Others such as Bengali Folk Tantra press my buttons and made me realize my magic is incredibly simple.

I'm an animist and a generator of energy so whilst I can work well in many spheres, for me finding a tradition and structure had become a very human need to find a place amongst others, rather than finding the right practice for myself.

As an artist who works in a number of differing mediums, could you describe something of your artistic process and how it may (or may not!) overlap with Magical work?

The more I immerse myself in my art the more I realize that art and magic are the same; expressions that can be directed. I don't plan anything that I do, just amass ingredients then when the time is right I go on automatic and channel the piece as it evolves. My creative process and magic run side by side, different facets of the same thing. The most conscious pieces that I make are charms, fetishes or elemental conductors and my larger pieces tend to be spirit houses or effect orientated portals, although often I don't realize what I've done until it is completed and the piece tells me.

For a long time, I was primarily working with bones and remnants of death as they were the most obvious conduits to certain characteristics or properties, but as I realized that everything has memory, I started working more with discarded and found objects and what was contained within them.

Spirit House by Charlotte Rodgers

In your (excellent) book The Bloody Sacrifice *you explore the way in which practitioners use their bodies to explore and create change; how has your own work with the body evolved since its publication?*

Hah! Hugely! I went through a very early menopause and my last period coincided with the completion of the book. Also, the book was written as my own blood was dealing with all the chemo that had been pumped into it to try and rid myself of Hep C and which took about two years to be expelled (the treatment didn't work).

Menopause is fascinating, and my energy is much more contained now. There is all the social stuff that goes with it... aging and perceived power loss etc., but in most ways my body is the strongest it has ever been.

I'm much more aware of the physical impact that magic has on me now, especially on my immune system (for people with long term hep c, your 50s is often the age it can really kick off and become problematic) and work with that.

I'm more careful about my body at magical gatherings as I find my metabolic rate goes into overdrive (this used to happen to me years ago, when I did readings for people) and I lose way too much weight and get run down.

Yoga is more important than ever for me and dance is a necessary joy.

I still regularly have ritualized tattoo work done on myself but mainly I am aware of an integration of my magickal self and my physical self that I think is a combination of my past work and perhaps just growing older and stronger in myself.

In many ways, my art work is intensely physical in that I am channelling part of myself into the art to bind it together and need to keep my back, hands and shoulders strong... if I want to channel I need to work with my physicality simply enough.

Family Dynamics (detail) by Charlotte Rodgers

Given your focus on the body and your use of animal remains in your Art, how well do you think contemporary Occultism is doing in its engagement with Death?

I'm not as much in the loop of what's going on in the occult community as I was... It seems that rituals of death and burial have progressed hugely, although I still think there is a great need of support for pagans and magickal practitioners after they have 'lost' someone. The acceptance in Western based occultism of ancestor worship has helped a lot, but I think many feel their beliefs are challenged when someone they love dies and could do with support that is non-denominational and unconditional, but still essentially magickal.

There is still a fascination with darkness and death in certain sections of Occultism that is perhaps blinkered but that is the nature of working with taboo... easier to go for the dark and forbidden rather than something like unconditional love and joy! (I can say this I think because I've had that struggle myself!)

Over the last few years there have been some deaths of people who were incredibly important to me magickally, Michael Howard, Donald Kraig and David Blank. There have also been important practitioners who have died that I've not had direct personal involvement with and it is worth thinking how their lives and deaths have contributed to the growth and development of the present magickal current, and what changes will occur in it due to their loss.

Lastly, can I ask what your hopes are for the future evolution of both your Magical and Artistic practices?

Now there's a question. Recently I've felt a need to go slow (not my usual way!) and make no major decisions.

The world is very crazy with major changes going on, so treading careful seems to be the best option.

I've started worked more, both magickally and creatively, with rust and discarded modern objects, and finding with ways to integrate it with nature and 'the old ways' to bring forth a progressive evolution.

I'd briefly touched on this in 2011 when I integrated broken glass from the London riots and car accidents into sculptures trying to positively redirect the rage and impotence at the injustice that fuelled these riots.

Now it seems the right time to carry on with this modern alchemy!

Aside from that I'm in the process of a final edit of The Fulcrum Method, a divinatory system that I've created with Roberto Migliussi, and also organising a Summer Solstice based exhibition in Bath, 'Rust, Blood and Bone'.

What I want in the long term and general sense? To carry on progressing with my art and magick, to carry on learning and to have fun.

I want to retain that joy in adventuring spiritually and creatively whilst not getting bogged down by games and infighting and power plays. I'd love to be able to make a living out of what I do, so I can focus all my attention on it and see how far I can take the journey, and to where.

Thanks very much Charlotte.

To see more of Charlotte's works, you can visit
her blog: https://charlottejane2002.wordpress.com/
and her gallery: https://charlotte-rodgers-caya.squarespace.com/

Wisdom in the Aeon of Maat

In reflecting upon the Aeon of Maat and how Nema's own work developed the initial articulation by Frater Achad, I feel one of her wisest insights relates to the importance of "the double current" in seeking to develop a more balanced magical path. In contrast to simply seeing our current age as needing the mono-message of Thelema or Will, Nema's own journey has been towards a place where the overlapping Aeons of Horus and Maat dialogue with each other.

Horus; "Welcome!" Ma'at; "In peace."

The issue of how Magicians in the West quantify progress has always been a tricky one. Yes, we may choose to rely on the grade system mapped out by a given Order that we participate in, but this is no guarantee of personal evolution. Grades and titles are not without value, but they seem to function primarily as markers of progress *within* the given sub-culture of that Order. I think a more interesting and potentially demanding question is how we translate any claimed maturation into social or cultural change.

Such dilemmas are not unique to overtly Gnostic or Magical religious paths, with most religions having to grapple with the more collective or political dimensions of their original spiritual message. Certainly in the Buddhist tradition the historical development of the Mahayana tradition (from the earlier Theravardan) reflects an attempt to explore the more collective implications of that philosophy.

The pursuit of true will as a project for the contemporary Mage certainly resonates with the existential and individualistic concerns of the 20th century that birthed Thelema, but is it enough? The icon of Horus as the conquering child certainly seems to capture the type of surging technological change of the last century, but to my mind this energy needs some counter-balance.

The primary symbolism in ancient Egypt regarding the goddess Maat reflect her position as the neter (divine principle) of justice and balance. The hieroglyph of the feather is seen as representing the breath of life, as well as the standard against which the human heart will be weighed at the judgement. Her other symbol of the ruler is in keeping with these ideas of accuracy, assessment and truth.

For Nema (and Achad) the importance of the Horus/Maat "double current" is that it at once acknowledges the need for a prophetic cleansing of a corrupt Piscean/Osirian age, while at the same time recognizing that such change needs balance and stabilization in order to prevent "Will" becoming egoic megalomania. I see great parallels between Maat and the Gnostic Sophia as the embodiment of wisdom. The punk rock energy of Horus may get the revolution started, but in the longer term we need our Aeons to overlap and to allow a multiplicity of perspectives to support us in the cultivation of a fairer society.

This idea of the Aeons being sequential and dominated by mono-mythologies is frequently promoted in esoteric lore, and while it may have been helpful and even accurate in times past, I believe that the value of such an approach is now limited. What Nema seems to be pointing towards (and which Maat herself embodies) is the importance of allowing these differing Aeonic currents to dance with and inform each other, and create what she describes as a "PanAeonic Magick".

In my view Pete Carroll highlights something similar in his seminal "Mass of Chaos B":

> In the first aeon, I was the Great Spirit
> In the second aeon, Men knew me as the Horned God, Pangenitor Panphage
> In the third aeon, I was the dark one, the Devil
> In the fourth aeon, Men knew me not, for I am the Hidden One
> In this new aeon, I appear before you as Baphomet

> The God before all gods who shall endure to the end
> Of the Earth.
>
> *Liber Null and Psychonaut*, p132

In contrast to those ages ruled by a singular narrative or dominant discourse, now is the time of Baphomet, a deity more overtly borne of humanity's creative imagination. Baphomet embodies duality itself and transcends it, within their being they hold the ongoing process of dissolving and coming together.

This concept of multiple Aeons was something I got turned onto during my year-long tenure as a member of the Temple of Set. While I decided not to continue as a member with the Temple's walls, I continue to gain great benefit from their articulation of the "Aeonic Words" that have been expressed by those members reaching the grade of Magus. The inauguration of the Temple and the Aeon of Set was brought about by Michael Aquino's receiving of the word *Xeper* ("become") in 1975, but since that time, other words such as *Runa* (Mystery), *Remanifest* and *Arkte* (respect for the animal realm) have been received. These words are all to be understood against the wider backdrop of the Temple's understanding of the Left-Hand path and the meta-project of self-awakening, but in my view they illustrate an evolving process toward a deeper exploration of what such work might entail.

I believe the Aeon of Maat with its core message of balance holds within it the possibility of the multiple, and the aspiration of being able to recognize numerous perspectives and approaches. Nema's artistic depiction of N'Aton captures much of this as the half of their face that is visible contains a multitude of individuals dwelling in a futuristic city scape. N'Aton represents the potentiality of a future in which dualities are played with by the Magician: transcended, discarded, redefined and embraced in accordance with a true will that balances both individual freedom and collective responsibility.

The icon of N'Aton provides a potential map for the Magician's project of self-sovereignty. N'Aton seeks to balance the needs for individual self-definition and collective connection. Rather than getting overly focused the type of brittle, self-obsession that can tip into solipsism or megalomania, for me N'Aton asks that any claims to insight are pressure tested in the realm of wider society. In many ways the Aeon of Maat closely parallels the description of the Aquarian age as described one of Nema's magical colleagues Louise Martinie of the New Orleans Voodoo Spiritual Temple:

> *The Aeon in which we are presently incarnate has been called by various names. "Aquarian" seems to be the designation which is most widely used in the New World cultures. The Aquarian mode emphasizes profound searching, a reliance on experiential knowledge, and a uniting of diverse occult systems. Aeonic Voodoo seeks to incorporate these dispositions in its structure.*
>
> **Waters of Return, p4**

He then goes on to describe this Aeon's defining features:

> *Anarchism; the state of being without a "frozen" hierarchy. Postdrogeny; the abrogation of all existent gender roles so that new perceptions may*

manifest. Feminism; as it is in the forefront in its stand against restriction and for human liberation. Equalitarianism; the belief that all people have equal political and social rights, and Nonviolence; a refusal to subject the self or others to physical coercion.

Ibid.

Whether we define this Aeon as being Aquarian, of Maat, or holding a multiplicity of overlapping words, we seem to be moving towards a place where language and definitions are being asked to become more plastic and amorphous in trying to stay alive to the diversity of human experience.

Thoughts on the Queerness of Gnosis

It's probably not very surprising that I find myself reflecting upon how Queerness and Gnosis intersect, given the importance they play in my life. Most of my writing bears witness to my attempt to explore the complexity of human life and how we utilize experiences of direct knowing in our attempts to manage the dilemma of existence.

While others may view the conflating of Queer experience and Gnosticism as being a personal eccentricity or indulgence on my part, I would ask for your patience as I try to unpack some of the resonances that I experience. For me the starting point of both the Queer-identified and the Gnostic is a sense of discomfort and dislocation in response to binary attempts at classification.

While the Gnostics are often typified as dualists, I would say that a large part of what lies at the heart of gnostic exploration is dissatisfaction with attempts to divide our experience of the world along binary lines. An orthodoxy that seeks to classify things in terms of the works of God or those of Satan made little sense to those religious free-thinkers who wanted to embrace complexity more fully. Rather than being satisfied with the simple answers of faith, the Gnostic sets out into deep space in order to explore the tension, complexity and contradiction that seems to lie at the heart of life's mystery.

The Gnostic is the sacred scientist in the truest sense in their attempts to openly explore; question and pressure test their findings. Their metaphysical insights may fail to meet the rigor of the strict reductionist, but their attempt to map the weird cosmologies experienced through inner perception still provide us with much of value. These strange inner landscapes had a clear resonance with depth psychologists such as Carl Jung, as he felt that they provided insight into the nature of human experience and how we might work with the process of personal transformation.

Beyond the Rainbow

Early Gnostic cosmologies such as those mapped out by early groups, for instance the Sethians and Valentinians, contain a wide variety of spiritual couplings (or syzygies) that seek to convey the dynamic dance at work in the process of creation. For the Gnostic, the numinous realm is full of a wide array of beings such as Aeons, Archons, Powers and Principalities, all vying for expression and manifestation into matter and the realm of human consciousness. While diagrammatic attempts to depict such systems usually come off looking quite linear, in reading the oft-confusing description of them in primary Gnostic texts, the heavenly host feels far more fluid, over-lapping and multi-directional.

To me, the Gnostics embody a type of heretical free-thinking that seeks to challenge a form of certainty that relies on blinkered tunnel-vision. Neat delineations that require us to ignore the messy complexity of our deepest longings are challenged by the heretics' brave act of choosing. While the pedlars of certainty proclaim loudly that their polarized, black and white world is either the result of natural order or God's will, the heretic is listening to a quieter inner voice.

The awakening to Queerness can of course happen in a whole host of ways. It might be an internal awareness of the complexity of desire or (as was in my case) communication from the straight world of the demiurge that my way of presenting was not working for them! These realizations may happen suddenly or in a more slow-burn fashion in which you become increasingly aware of dissonance. Whichever speed it happens at, this is a profound unfolding of who we sense we are and in my case it definitely had a Gnostic dimension. If the admonition to "Know Thyself" was to have authenticity, then it needed to account for the outsider experience that I experienced as a Queer person.

Gnostic explorers of most stripes are usually willing to question what we mean by the natural. In trying to grapple with the discomfort associated with our experience of living, they sought to question the narratives about this transmitted by Church and State. These organs of authority have been keen to get us to believe all sorts of ideas, in the name of their being natural. Whether it's the inevitability of reproduction, the subjugation of women or the exclusion of black people, both Church and State have the potential to become archonic in their restriction of personal expression and liberty. In their attempt to control and contain, they seek to minimize the complexity of our life experience and to present a dominant narrative that limits the possibility of a deeper connection based on a truly rich diversity.

The syzygies so loved by the Gnostics often sought to embody a richer story in which the binaries experienced were held together as they moved through a process of reconciliation. Manifestations of this unification pop-up in androgynous figures such as Adam Kadmon or Abraxas, but I think that we risk losing something crucial if we see them as fixed icons and fail to appreciate the Queer dynamism that they embody. Queerness presents a disruptive challenge to our attempts at neatness. At best it moves beyond mere hip theorizing and compels us to enact, perform and intensify the blurry reality of who we are.

In this fluid dance, Queerness can be experienced as identity, mood and the dynamic that exists in the interactions between people, objects and organization. For me it provides a way of knowing that provides not only a space for inhabiting the present, but as we have considered, it also provides us with a lens for viewing the past. In asking us to stay awake to sensitivity to context and process, Queerness provides a necessary challenge to the type of brittleness that can come when we get overly invested in fixed identities. In my view, such a dynamic creates a type of optimism as I see glimpses of the type of human creativity that José Esteban Muñoz refers to as "Futurity".

I have already spoke of the inspiration that I have gained via Nema's description of N'Aton as an embodiment of our future magical selves, and part of my attraction to this figure is in the way it manifests a type of magical optimism and Futurity. Depictions of N'Aton often hold together the individual and collective perspectives and such images embody a type of spiritual awakening that allows for a multiplicity of perspective. When we step away from the tunnel-vision of either Christian or Orthodox Thelemic eschatology, we can begin to explore the Queer possibility of our aeonic utopias overlapping, blurring with and potentially strengthening each other as they balance and inform each other's insights.

This is a tightrope walk in which we try to balance the reality of our individual and collective struggles with the need to explore the possibility of what hope might mean. When the Archons shout their "truth" so loudly, we must dare to keep the richness of our stories alive! I'll end with this great quote from Sara Ahmed in which they discuss the possibility of what we might create when we radically reappraise the type of future we might have:

> *To learn about possibility involves a certain estrangement from the present. Other things can happen when the familiar recedes. This is why affect aliens can be creative: not only do we want the wrong things, not only do we embrace possibilities that we have been asked to give up, but we create life worlds around these wants. When we are estranged from happiness, things happen. Hap [sic] happens.*
>
> ***The Promise of Happiness*, p218**

Androgynes: Then, Now and Not Yet

Introduction

Most people get to know that they are Queer from quite an early age. In my case it was not something I knew innately. Initially it was something that my world told me about.

I was probably 6 when my Dad returned from a trip to Scotland where he had been working as a bricklayer. He had returned with gifts: a big yellow digger for me and a Scottish dancing doll for my younger sister. I remember clearly the moment when, after receiving our presents, my sister and I looked across at each other and simply swapped!

As I recollect my early years and adolescence, there were a number of such occasions when it became all too apparent that I was out of step. Maleness in my world came with some fairly fixed markers of success and I as far as I could tell I wasn't doing so well. I didn't even know what a "poof" was, but I could guess from the mockery with which it was spat that it was probably something to hide.

It can be easy to get shut down by shame. While I am certainly aware of situations and groups of people that I avoided due to their perception that my gender expression didn't fit with their norms, thankfully this was not the whole of the story. While the question of whether magicians are born or made is open to debate, I managed to find conduits for letting my Queer magic flow.

I have already spoken of the impact that Hatha yoga practice had on not only shaping my metaphysical outlook but also my relationship to my body. Like Billy Elliott's answer to the question that he was asked at his ballet school audition: "What do you feel when you are dancing?" Billy answers that he forgets himself and feels like electricity. This makes sense to me and the way in which the opening extension of the asanas allowed me to more fully inhabit my physical self and the possibility of the sensual.

If yoga touched my body, then it was music that allowed me to access my creative, emotional self. I remember flicking through a friend's record collection and seeing Bowie's *Scary Monsters* and some of the early Devo albums. Yes the music moved me, but much more than that, these strange New Wave icons seemed to inhabit a sexless space in which gender seemed endlessly plastic and subject to mutation. Bowie's make-up and hair unsettled and inspired me in equal measure as the alien persona of Major Tom strutted through my increasingly rich internal world.

Back then I didn't possess a word to capture that strange blurring of male and female, all I knew was that I liked what I saw and that it acted as a mirror in which to see something that I knew was deeply real about myself. The concepts of androgyny and Queerness were to come much later, but in having my imagination captured by the gender ambiguity of the New Wave and the New Romantic, it felt as though an internal radar had been activated that sensitized me to these presentations that challenged the binary norm. I offer these reflections with a deep bow of gratitude to early Duran Duran, Depeche Mode and the orange buzz-cut of Annie Lennox!

My adolescent exposure to androgynous imagery was not only limited to my musical world, it was spiritual as well. Having spent most of my teenage years wandering around the Gold Coast area in Australia I had been exposed to all sorts of religious weirdness. I remember the hours spent moving between music shops and the Hare Krishna restaurant at which I was able to acquire free books and magazines that fuelled my yogic imagination. In addition to discovering the joys of mantra meditation, these magazines contained some beautiful depictions of the 16th century Vaishnava saint, Lord Caitanya.

Caitanya was a bhakti yoga mystic whose intensity of love for Krishna took him into some decidedly Queer territory. In seeking to express the degree of his love for his Lord, he often dressed as Krishna's divine partner Radha. This act of sacred cross-dressing typified the ecstatic longing that Caitanya was able to direct in helping reform Vaishnava spirituality. Some view him as an incarnation of Krishna and if we at least entertain that notion, we are presented with a deeply tantric manifestation whereby the power of devotion allows for both partners of a divine coupling to be held within one being.

If it was the beautifully ambiguous portraits of Caitanya that drew me to him, my relationship with Jesus came more through words and story. Having not grown up in a religious home, apart from the Lord's prayer I was largely unaware of the Gospel stories. This was to change dramatically during my mid-teens, as the certainties of Evangelical Christianity were to provide a ready conduit through which to pour my adolescent longing for identity.

The depiction of Jesus in the Gospels provided me with a model of masculinity that accommodated a sense of gentleness and emotional openness that I found liberating. The Christ to which I became devoted not only cleared the Temple, but also went seeking for the one lost sheep.

Leonardo da Vinci, Salvator Mundi, detail. 1500

As I look back now, 30 years later, I am struck by the homoerotic edge that seemed to pervade so much of my spiritual devotion at that time. The Church at which I worshipped was decidedly conservative in terms of it theology and views on homosexuality, but seemed quite comfortable with hours being spent in writhing ecstasy before the throne of a Messiah who in my mind's eye was a beautiful, bearded 33-year-old male who was deeply in love with me! One might be forgiven for getting confused.

Such paradoxes permeated the Charismatic/Pentecostal form of worship that I engaged in. On the one hand they adopted an attitude towards sexual pleasure that was quite severe and repressive (sex outside of marriage being wrong and masturbation being viewed as morally dubious); and yet theirs was an embodied ecstasy, where God as Holy Spirit induced dance, shaking, speaking in tongues and all manner of strange "signs and wonders".

While I can now see this radical sublimation as potentially harmful to many, I remain unclear whether it was entirely so for me. As a person who finds comfort in the blurry self-descriptors of gender fluidity and grey asexuality, this location of spiritual experience within the physical body allowed me to access a more polymorphous type of sensuality that seemed far less located in genital sexuality or inherited scripts regarding the erotic activity I should be engaged in to prove my normality.

Although my current spiritual path is evidence that this form of belief failed to meet my needs, I can see direct parallels between that past and my current use of dance, music and other body-transforming practices. Even if the certainties of adolescent belief no longer feel authentic, in the day-to-day practice that informs my ongoing spiritual explorations I still feel the powerful pull of devotion and a desire to experience an ecstasy in the body that blurs the lines between Agape and Eros. Even with my conscious embrace of theological uncertainty, I dance, shake, drum and burst forth with strange tongues as I walk the tight-rope liminal zone that my life asks me to inhabit.

Androgyny as Spiritual Ideal

It will come as no surprise that in my view, Queerness and a gnostic approach to religious exploration have considerable overlaps. It is my belief that our experience of being an "Outsider" can be encountered in a number of different aspects of our lives at any given moment and that insights gained or progress made can benefit the wider story of how we live and experience our lives.

The concept of Androgyny as a religious aspiration can be found in a multitude of cultural settings and across a vast period of time. Authors such as June Singer and Mircea Eliade have produced highly valuable work documenting the wide range of spiritual contexts that have sought to explore Androgyny as an expression of cosmological wholeness and as a goal of personal integration.

Geographically it spans across pretty much the entire globe and encompasses traditions as diverse as Tantra, Judaic Kabbalah, Hermetic Alchemy and a variety of Native animistic traditions. Eliade highlights that the employment of the Androgyne as an organizing idea has an enduring resonance due to the way it simultaneously points toward the primal unity of opposites (often in a numinous pre-history), while at the same time trying to map the process of human development. Part of its ongoing appeal seems to be the way in which it seeks to hold in parallel our Gnostic longings concerning divinity and our own experience of psychological transformation. The wholeness of all binaries held in tension within a single being offering us the hope that our own ennui will be soothed via our own internal marriage of opposites.

In her seminal *Women, Androgynes, and Other Mythical Beasts* Wendy Doniger O'Flaherty goes some way in identifying the possible range of androgynous forms as represented in religious and mythical iconography. In this highly valuable work she examines the Androgyne as a manifestation of aspirational unity, "fusing", as depicted by Ardhanarishvara (the composite form of Shiva and Parvati as one form), and of chaos, "splitting", such as the differentiation enacted via puberty rituals. The ideal of fusing can be seen as having many resonances with Jung's goal of integrating the contrasexual self (Anima/Animus); while the desire for reverting to an undifferentiated pre-creation has some parallels to Freud's primal wish for death.

In trying to garner such an overview we will always struggle to contain the complexity of such a topic, as it seeks to engage with both the mythic archetype and the lived reality of how gender non-conformity is manifested in day to day human existence. While the highly balanced "vertical" androgyny of Ardhanarishvara may represent an iconographic and aspirational success as an embodiment of fusing, the messier, potentially more monstrous movement in, out and back through multiple identities may hold as much value, as manifestations of how we actually live with the tensions of binaries. Those trickster stories of amputated penises and ecstatic cross-dressing may come closer to embodying the type of embraced imperfection, or Jack Halberstein's concept of "Queer failure", that makes our lives more possible. As he says:

> *Failure can become a potent form of critique, a repudiation of capitalism and profit margins, a refusal of the norm, an indifference to assimilation and a route to other ways of being in the world.*
>
> **Jack Halberstein, Embrace Queer Failure, at http://www.jackhalberstam.com/ll/**

The Androgyne has a vital role in pointing us towards the occult, the enigmatic and the hidden. Its weird complexity offers not only the possibility of transcendence of the erotic (the nullified eunuch) but also the danger of Eros unchecked by the natural limitation of childbirth. In the projected fantasies of its viewer, the hermaphrodite's complex sexual possibility is at once potentially alluring and terrifying. To engage with them may result in a cornucopia of new sensual experiences and/or our ultimate destruction via their alien genitalia. They become avatars of Baphomet in being both sex and death, our dissolving and coming back together.

The Eunuch as an androgyne also presents us with a type of dialogic tension in which story and fantasy intersect. Via their various degrees of genital nullification they may represent a state of idealized asexuality or a perfect servant who while safely sterile is also the potential recipient of other people's penetrative activity. The chaste harem attendant and Hijra sex worker represent the extremes of this dichotomy, but in both cases they hold a magic in that their very presence is potentially unsettling and disruptive.

In the gospel of Matthew, Jesus made the observation:

For there are eunuchs who were born that way from their mother's womb; and there are eunuchs who were made eunuchs by men; and there are also eunuchs who made themselves eunuchs for the sake of the kingdom of heaven. He who is able to accept this, let him accept it.

Matthew 19:12

Androgynes, whether of nature or of human creation, disturb our perception of what we think of as natural. If we also account for the broad range of folks who would embrace some form of transgender identity we also see a vast number of possible responses (changes pursued in external presentation, surgery, hormones and psychology). The magical potential of the Androgyne lies in the sense of uncertainty that they induce. This sense of liminality may attract or repel depending on our own level of comfort around self-exploration, and our ability to sit with not knowing. Often this feels connected to the distance between Androgyny as an idealized spiritual icon and the messier reality of the Androgyne as a Queer embodiment. This lived experience feels richer, more complex and a more creative expression of individual creativity.

Standing Ardhanari c.1800

Exercise: Ardhanarishvara brain rewiring rite

Purpose:

The purpose of this working is to use ritual practice in order to help us tune into the energies of the divine androgyny and to assist us in gaining a greater sense of balance and integration within ourselves.

Equipment:

Pen and Paper (for constructing sigil).

Music for dancing.

Materials for constructing an altar to the divine Androgyne.

Commit to a minimum of 15 minutes per day for a week, in order to undertake the contemplative practice and the sigil-launching rite.

Method:

1. Firstly we will construct an altar to the principle of the divine Androgyne. You may adapt an existing altar, or construct a fresh one. The altar may be as simple or elaborate as you wish and may benefit from images of Androgyny found in both mythic depictions and in contemporary culture. It may take some time to find the component parts. Stay open to adding new elements as the work proceeds.
2. Construct a sigil to Ardhanarishvara. There are lots of ways to construct these magical pictograms, but usually we remove any repeated letters and then arrange the remaining ones into a shape that appeals to us. The aim here is to create a symbol that can become an object of focus and contemplation.

3. Place your sigil at the centre of your altar and then for the next seven days use this sculpted space as an object of contemplation/veneration. Deploy those practices such as mantra work, mindfulness practice, the offering of incense etc. as a means of creating a connection to the concept of the divine Androgyne as a balancing/integrating force.
4. On the evening of the seventh day (if you can get this to coincide with a cool phase of the moon all the better), prepare your ritual space in order to allow some dancing and get your music ready.
5. During your chosen dance track (I chose "I Feel Love", by Donna Summer), I'd like you to visualize the sigil in the hemisphere of your brain that co-ordinates your non-dominant hand. So, if you are predominantly right-handed, visualize it in the right hemisphere which co-ordinates your left hand. Dance your dance while visualizing the sigil!
6. As you dance visualize your sigil being absorbed by your brain's non-dominant hemisphere.

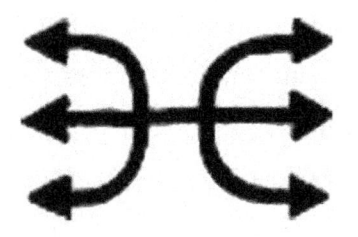

7. In order to create balance and integration between the hemispheres, visualize a double-ended trident lying horizontally across your brain. This piece of gnostic machinery will allow the energy of the absorbed sigil to move between the

two hemispheres of the brain allowing new connections and balance to be formed. At the mid-point of your chosen music, visualize the sigil in both spheres of your brain.

8. Stop dancing when your track ends, and give thanks at your altar. Spend time rubbing your hands together and gently massaging the sides of your face and body—this will allow you to ground yourself at the end of the ritual and reduce any sense of imbalance.

9. Thank yourself for doing this work to nurture and develop yourself. Some people like to destroy the physical basis of their sigil at this point as a means of acknowledging the launching of this specific endeavour and marking an ending to this phase of the working. Continue using your altar as a focal point for this work for as long as it pleases you.

Witches dancing with devils, featured in The History of Witches and Wizards *(1720)*

Monstrous Alchemy

The impact of Queer experience on the ideal of Androgyny is a truly disruptive one. Gone are our neat Kabbalistic flow charts and clear-cut Neoplatonic stages of descent. In contrast to these linear sequences, this Queered Androgyny is an ever oscillating, multi-directional chaos-star whose many rays can be simultaneously moving outward in expression and engagement, and inward in reflection and self-nurture.

This principle of Androgyny is fed as much by the lived experience of unique, individual Androgynous people as it is by the realm of aspirational metaphysics. It as much about creativity of the Radical Faery and Butch Lesbian as it about Adam Kadmon or Ardhanarishvara. For me, to work with this form of Androgyny means to acknowledge a dialectical process that seeks to capture the world of ideal forms, while at the same time experiencing a dialogical reality in which a multitude of positions need to be held together without a necessary resolution.

To seek deep benefit in engaging with these ideas and images seems to require that we tolerate a certain degree of uncertainty. So often this form of doubt, confusion and psychological tension is seen as negative, a hindrance to spiritual development, and yet I believe this does not need to be case. For those of us seeking to walk an occult path, we are regularly called upon to make use of emotions and methods which our exoteric cousins view as dangerous or retrograde. If however we are able to engage consciously with the sense of resistance experienced in grappling with the complexity of such dialogues, this very tension can bring about alchemical change.

If the stated aim of magical work is to create change, it would seem somewhat odd to then resist the transformation when it comes; and yet in my own life this has so often been the case. Change can happen at many levels and impact how we experience ourselves and engage in relationships with others. The routes to change can be manifested in dilemmas, loss and conflict, and the keys we need are to be found in attending to the strangeness of our dreams and the currents of the unconscious made manifest in our Art.

This is the unconscious territory that the Surrealists were so adept in exploring in their work, with the strange, frequently jarring images revealing aspects of self that were bizarre, blurred and monstrous. In alchemical terms this connection to the unconscious and the shadow represent the stage of *nigredo* or "blackening". For the surrealists such territory was vital to their artistic inspiration and similarly for our magical work to have any really depth or sustained power, we must tap into this libidinal black flame of inspiration.

We have already explored something of the fertile intersect that exists between Surrealism and the artistic deployment of occult ideas and images. Themes as diverse as the etheric double, the daemonic and the Witches' Sabbath were explored to varying degrees and there seems to be a significant connection between this use of magical themes and the weird animalistic characters with which they populated their artistic landscapes.

The link between the magical, the animal and the potentially Queer is present in much Surrealist work and for me the most engaging aspects of such exploration lies in the way in which it tries to communicate that zone of liminal strangeness and mystery. The Surrealist imagination was alive to potency to be found in understanding the animal (whether actual or in more mythic forms) as a way of recontacting the sensual and instinctual realms that weave through the body. This wilder magic seems to connect to a pre-verbal stage of development that resonates with Spare's idea of "atavistic resurgence".

The folklore of the lycan and vampyre point us towards a magical worldview in which we can explore the vitality gained through a deeper connection to the visceral. Similarly the Witches' animal familiar and the "fetch" or animal-dimension of Norse soul-lore, breach our polite attempts to conceive of a humanity devoid of wildness.

In contrast to the clean, vertical fusing of Ardhanarishvara, the truly Queer genius of Levi's depiction of Baphomet is partly located in the way in which the animal is integrated alongside the male and female. In trying to work with our own processes of dissolving and coming back together, Baphomet's animal dimensions remind us of the power, joy and danger that can be accessed when we risk tuning into the whole of ourselves.

My own attempts to access these states has come via body-work, dance/shaking states and prolonged trance drumming. I have also had a great deal of pleasure revisiting Gordon MacLellan's book *Sacred Animals* which provides some excellent practical guidance for exploring these themes. The ability to inhabit these places feels vital for those of us seeking to embody freethinking and the magic of the Queer. These places beyond binaries and old certainties rarely allow prolonged rest, but they are undoubtedly transformational!

Surreal Witchcraft

The nocturnal dream journeys of the Witch embody a cognitive liberty that refuses to be imprisoned despite the efforts of the authoritarian oppressor. However they might seek to enforce their orthodoxies or to harm and torture the body, the spirit of the Witch struggled hard in refusing the limitation of their chains. To my mind, these heretical heroes were seen as threatening due to the way in which they embodied a more authentic and visceral humanity, connected to the sexual and the wild.

The sabbatic revelries of the Witch were located as much in the projections of their oppressors as they were in actual practice, and yet even here we can sense the potency and strangeness of the unconscious realm. The fevered imaginings of *Malleus Maleficarum* reflect a sadism born of suppression. I cannot help but see the reports of the inquisitors as a distorted mirror image of the type of freedom that they secretly longed for: "If I could do anything, I would like to..."

The depictions of the Witches' Sabbath are typically simultaneously sensual and grotesque. They are conclaves of perversity and yet in their depiction they often unconsciously capture a male gaze that holds both disgust and longing. Such images seem to reflect the sense of internal conflict at work in the inquisitorial eye, and the potentially queering, alchemical impact that such perceptions of perversity can induce. In her work *Queer Phenomenology*, Sarah Ahmed observes:

> *Perversion is also a spatial term, which can refer to the wilful determination to counter or go against orthodoxy, but also to what is wayward and thus "turned away from what is right, good and proper.*
>
> *For some queer theorists, this is what makes "the perverse" a useful starting point for thinking about the "disorientations" of queer, and how it can contest not only heteronormative assumptions, but also social conventions and orthodoxies in general.*
>
> **Queer Phenomenology, p78**

Hans Baldung Grien: Die Hexen 16th century

Surreal Witchcraft

The archetype of the Witch is innately bonded to the queer, the twisted and the perverse. In its raw nocturnal sensuality it challenges attempts at control and it organizes itself into cells of practice for those bold enough to seek their own power and self-definition outside of the bounds of convention. The possible/partial etymology of *Wicce* being "to twist" or bend, points toward the wilful pursuit of a non-straight and less linear approach.

The Witch is the dream dweller par excellence and as such they provide us (whether we are Witch identified or not) with a form of surreal inspiration that when embraced allows the possibility of greater queerness and greater self-transformation. To gain access to this realm, we must dare the lucid sleep where we utilize the less-filtered reality of our dreams.

The character of the Witch within the Surrealist canon is probably embodied most vividly in the work of Leonora Carrington. We have already considered the centrality of her work in manifesting that strange space between dreams and waking, male and female, real and surreal. For me her work pushes hard against the attempts of orthodoxy to contain and control the power of the female imagination.

For Carrington, the Witch embodies the figure willing to bend and distort the known and the orthodox. The richness of her many years in Mexico provided her with a vibrant example of how to meld the Catholicism of her upbringing with her own, deeper magical impulses. Her time spent with curandera and in exploring the mythology of pre-conquest beliefs of the Maya, inspired her own journey in synthesizing both Catholic and Celtic/Native British currents; as Susan Aberth observes:

> *This combination of the heretical with the orthodox exemplifies the multiplicity of belief systems the artist is dedicated to preserving as part of the suppressed history of female spirituality.*
>
> ***Leonora Carrington: Surrealism, Alchemy and Art**,* p126

In exploring the power of the Witch, Carrington depicts the magical circle and the kitchen as locations able to sit within the same space. For Carrington it feels that her work as a magician dissolves any dualism between artistic creation, nurture and sorcerous realms. When pursuing such integration, the visible and invisible, the known and the occult interpenetrate each other as a manifestation of a truly earthed divinity:

> *By transforming the domestic table into a sacramental altar Carrington creates a feminine sacred space that links worlds, providing access to multiple states of consciousness while collapsing the hierarchies that have prevented a more inclusive vision of spiritual possibilities.*
>
> **Ibid.**

The nocturnal realm of the Witch is one in which the quiet of night's darkness allows us more space to tune in. With day's labour done, the hearth invites us to rest, engage and feel the edges of the coming dream-sleep. This is the place that the Witch beckons to; a place where the busy cognitions of bright sunlight are left to simmer.

Carrington's work depicts a form of alchemy truly plugged in to chthonic power. Her Witchcraft rejects a false dichotomy between folk-magical practice and the depths of spiritual transformation. For her the Celtic sídhe that inhabit much of her work are the spirits of the earth and, the holders of alchemy's secrets. With the incoming of a Roman Christianity hellbent on homogenization, the old gods choose to go underground and inhabit those mounds (literally, "sídhe") that still hold such allure for those drawn to the serpentine energy of the land. If we risk reconnection to such power, transformation becomes possible in a way that rejects false dualities and allows creation from a place of deep rootedness.

A Puja for Heretical Heroes

As we approach the end of this stage of our journey together, I thought it would be good to create some guidelines for an exercise that I hope will help you to take forward some of the ideas that we have been exploring. Our first exercise involved the construction of a Heretic's Altar with a view to it helping us identify those people and principles that help our own sense of spiritual freethinking. Hopefully this altar (whether actual or constructed in your mind palace) has become an anchor point for this work and the collages, cut-ups and sigils that you created were able to inhabit and inform this space.

This final exercise takes the form of a puja or act of veneration in which we give thanks and acknowledge those powers that continue to inspire us on our path to gnosis. To worship is not necessary (though you can if you like!), it is enough that you notice and embrace those things that will empower you in moving forward and drawing in your most excellent magical self. You may choose to offer incense or music, you may wish to speak your thanks out loud into the quiet of the room; whichever means you choose, be sure to give thanks to both them and yourself for getting this far.

In addition to activity and verbiage make sure you leave space for silence. Activities like mindfulness practice and silent meditation provide us with the space needed to fuel our cognitive liberty. Such space allows us to question the narratives we have inherited and to let go of the one that we continually write for ourselves. Such stories can provide us with shape and meaning, but they can sometimes limit and domesticate our potential. With any luck our heretical heroes can help shake these stories up!

What follows is a piece of liturgical poetry that we use within the Zen Hearth meditation group I am involved in. You may wish to use it as part of your own puja process:

> We come seeking gnosis
> And the wisdom to apply it.
> We come seeking the Old Ways
> That we might truly live now
> And become the future.
>
> We come seeking the three realms
> And the three treasures
> Sky, Earth and Sea
> Our Gods, our Ancestors and the Spirits of Place.
>
> The World Tree is the realm of our practice:
>
> Our Minds, our Bodies and our Lives.
> We seek to take up the Runes
> Fragments of mystery
> As we see sense and nonsense
> On the road we travel.
>
> We seek to live and we seek to dream
>
> We are the edge dwellers for whom darkness and light must ever dance together

A Puja for Heretical Heroes

Both singular and collective
Isolate and connected
We are the ever-becoming ones!
We give thanks to the heroes of practice:
Heretics and Holy Fools.

We give thanks for the complex Web of Truth:
Help us to see multiplicity!

We give thanks to those who sit like mountains together.

Holy Mountains

Words Made Flesh

Being a human often involves the construction of stories. In trying to make sense of our own lives, those of other beings on the planet and the Universe more generally, we create narratives to help us order what might be going on. We respond to the information we receive and fuse it with our existing perspectives in order to make decisions about how we wish to live and the potential risks posed to our current experience of being alive. Most of the time we do this amazing work without even knowing that it is going on, but sometimes we have moments when we realize we are doing it, and we might want to make conscious changes to our method and style.

Most religious movements and schools of philosophy make claim to providing tools for waking us up from the automatic reliance on assumptions. The process of becoming aware of the lenses we rely on for viewing the world can be shocking and disorientating as we try to incorporate any new insights gained. The problems for most religions come when the incoming of new, enlightening knowledge (gnosis) begins to disrupt the presuppositions that they themselves rely on e.g. that God either doesn't exist or is radically different from how they were initially understood to be.

At the start of this book, we began thinking about how we think, and the risks involved in stepping outside the lines of received orthodoxy. If we start to question received truths and embrace the heretic's path of choosing our own way, we must realize that we will increase discomfort both for ourselves and those around us. For the freethinker, to refuse to question is an even less desirable, stultifying path, but we would be naïve if we underestimate the disruptive force of heretical thoughts and behaviour.

Part of the creative, disruptive power of the heretic, is that they take existing received truths and bend them. It would be bad enough if we adopted an antithetical position, but the fact that we take an image or language and inject it with a new, nuanced or odd meaning, truly infuriates those seeking to maintain their monopoly on perceived truth. The gnosis of the heretic triggers a creative process in which their artistry reveals strange variants of reality. While on one level we reject the easier answers of faith, we can retain a symbiotic relationship with those beliefs and images. In our heresy we internalize these ordered creeds and transform them in to something that is far stranger and far more interesting.

The adoption of such bold new readings allows the possibility of inhabiting a place of greater spaciousness that feels more congruent with the lives we wish to live. Such territory tends to be at the outer edges of familiar maps and requires a level of wit and will that many of us experience as demanding and exhilarating in equal measure.

While each of us need to discover our own optimum means for accessing spaces of cognitive liberty, I have noticed that my own is facilitated by allowing apparently disparate sources to sit alongside each other. In this book I have been aware of my own journey in allowing the different aspects of my personal religious history dialogue with each other. The Witch and the Cleric have been sitting down together for a beverage and conversation in the hope that new meaning might be discovered. All too often I have tried to rush them in the hope of a tidy resolution, but thankfully they have resisted my efforts!

In seeking to allow the unique parts of my own story to have a voice, I have found more help in dreams and art than I have in theological concepts and reformulations. Of course I find great value in thinking and writing, but they face the danger of overly concretizing those states that are more subtle, subjective and sensed. In seeking to resist the urge to prematurely reconcile, synthesize or harmonize this multiplicity of voices and ideas, I have found that artistic experimentation within a ritual context is a powerful tool.

Stages of Life *by Bartholomeus Anglicus, 1486*

While others may gain greater stimulus via extended textual analysis and linear debate, on their own these have not been enough to allow me to access the type of psychological integration that I long for. The Queer and transformative states that I need in order to challenge the bulwarks of orthodoxy in my own life have been found more readily in the images of Abraxas, Baphomet and N'Aton than in attempts at systematic theology. I consider that these part-made gods embody the ongoing dialogue between idealized androgyny and the complexity of Queer experience. The Queer aspirations of "Postdrogyny" and "Pandrogyne" are the first fruits of an artistic exploration of the possibility of identity. This is an Aquarian age in which our neat categories are troubled and disrupted by the bold lives of those seeking a more authentic way.

The exercises in this book that have made use of sigils, collage and altar sculpts have all been ways of allowing us to inhabit a type of magical space allowing for a personal alchemy that I hope will catalyse change on a wider, societal level. This zone is the place of the crossroads, and as I have observed elsewhere:

> *If we journey to the crossroads in our attempt to rediscover our magic, we are inevitably entering a realm of liminal possibility. The crossroads is a meeting place of apparent opposites and seeming contradictions. The dynamic tension generated by the friction between these polarities makes it the place of initiation.*
>
> *A Gnostic's Progress*, p155

The crossroads is a place of incarnation and inspiration and the word must become flesh (John 1:14) in order for us to experience its fullness. May our art, inspiration and willingness to explore allow access to such fullness!

My hope is that this book has provided a degree of inspiration as you seek to find your way to greater liberty. This is rarely an easy peace, but as we allow ourselves to tune into the complexity and mystery of our lives, may all of us experience greater authenticity and freedom.

So Mote it Be!

Bibliography

Assagioli, R. (1990) *Psychosynthesis*, Crucible

Bateson, G. (1973) *Steps to an Ecology of Mind*, Granada

Brekke, D. (2010) *The Gnostics*, First Harvard University Press

Carroll, P. (1987) *Liber Null and Psychonaut*, Weiser

Carroll, P. (1992) *Liber Kaos*, Weiser

Cohn, N. (1975) *Europe's Inner Demons*, Sussex University Press

Csikszentmihalyi, M. (2002) *Flow Rider*

Churton, T. (1997) *The Gnostics*, Barner and Noble Press

Dunn, J. (1980) *Christology in the Making*, SCM

Ehrman, B. (2003) *Lost Scriptures*, Oxford University Press

Epperly, B. (2011) *Process Theology: A Guide for the Perplexed*, T&T Clark International

Flowers, S. (2006) *The Fraternitas Saturni*, Runa Raven Press

Flowers, S. (1996) *Hermetic Magic*, Weiser

Fries, J. (2009) *Seidways*, Mandrake

Gilbert, P. (2009) *The Compassionate Mind*, Constable

Glucklich, A. (1997) *The End of Magic*, Oxford University Press

Hutton, R. (1995) *The Triumph of the Moon*, Oxford University Press

Hoeller, S. (2014) *The Gnostic Jung and the Seven Sermons to the Dead*, Quest

Hoeller, S. (2002) *Gnosticism*, Quest

Jonas, H. (1963) *The Gnostic Religion*, Beacon Press

Jones, P. and Pennick, N. (1997) *A History of Pagan Europe*, Routledge

Leadbeater, C. (1920) *The Science of the Sacraments*, The St. Albans Press

Levine, P. (2015) *Trauma and Memory*, North Atlantic Books

Linehan, M. (1993) *Skills Training Manual for Treating Borderline Personality Disorder*, The Guilford Press

Lowe, V. (1985) *Alfred North Whitehead: The Man and His Work, Volume 1: 1861–1910*, The John Hopkins University Press

Kelly, M. (2009) *Apophis*, Blurb Books UK

Mason, Barry. (1993) "Human Systems: The Journal of Systemic Consultation &: Management. Vol. 4. 189–200" COLFTRC & KCC

MacLellan, G. (1997) *Sacred Animals*, Capall Bann Publishing

Michelet, J. (1965) *Satanism and Witchcraft*, Tandem

Nema. (1995) *Maat Magick*, Weiser

Ogilvy, G. (2006) *The Alchemist's Kitchen*, Wooden Books

Ouspensky, P. (1987) *In Search of the Miraculous*, Arkana

Pagels, E. (1979) *The Gnostic Gospels*, Weidenfield and Nicolson

Peck, M. S. (1990) *The Different Drum*, Arrow

Pratchett, T. (2008) *Small Gods*, Corgi

Satir, V. (1972) *Peoplemaking*, Science and Behaviour Books

Segal, R. (Ed.) (1995) *The Allure of Gnosticism*, Open Court

Singer, J. (2003) *A Gnostic Book of Hours*, Nicolas Hays

Smith, A.P. (2008) *The Gnostics*, Watkins Publishing

Bibliography

Trismegistus, H. (trans. Salaman et al 2001) *Corpus Hermeticum*, Duckbacks

Vayne, J. and Dee, S. (2014) *Chaos Craft*, The Universe Machine

Wyllie, T. (2009) *Love Sex Fear Death*, Feral House

Wyrd, N. and Vayne, J. (2012) *The Book of Baphomet*, Mandrake of Oxford

Made in the
USA
Monee, IL